Y0-BCD-791

INTEGRATING AMERICA'S HERITAGE

A Congressional Hearing to establish a National Commission on Negro History and Culture

Edited by Howard N. Meyer

Statements by:
James Baldwin
Roy Innis
Jackie Robinson
Senator Edward S. Brooke
and many others

McGrath Publishing Company
College Park, Maryland

This book is the substance of:

HEARING

BEFORE THE

SELECT SUBCOMMITTEE ON LABOR

OF THE

COMMITTEE ON EDUCATION AND LABOR HOUSE OF REPRESENTATIVES

NINETIETH CONGRESS

SECOND SESSION

ON

H.R. 12962

A BILL FOR THE ESTABLISHMENT OF A COMMISSION ON NEGRO HISTORY AND CULTURE

HEARING HELD IN NEW YORK, N.Y., MARCH 18, 1968

INTEGRATING AMERICA'S HERITAGE

By Howard N. Meyer

The Congressional power of investigation has a great and productive past. The need to inquire into an aspect of American economic or social life in order to legislate wisely is obvious; the peripheral function of informing all constituencies of facts by means of public hearing—and thereby incidentally arousing voters in districts of lawmakers insensitive to some evils—can lead to abuses, but is essentially legitimate.

Our abhorrence of the wrongs done to individuals and the propaganda for cold war objectives that have been the fruit of the many (probably unconstitutional for lack of legislative purposes) so-called "investigations" of subversives should not becloud the issue. It is well to remember that among the constructive and *bona fide* ones, the first of the truly great exercises of Congressional investigative power was the work of the Joint Committee on Reconstruction of the Thirty-ninth Congress; its fruit was the Fourteenth Amendment to the United States Constitution.

To recall the Joint Committee of 1865-66 in considering the Hearing of March 18, 1968 (on a Bill to Establish a Commission on Negro History and Culture) is appropriate because Congressman James H. Scheuer's Hearing called attention to the persistence of a great national evil and the need for a remedy, just as did the Hearings held in 1866 on the conditions in the "late rebel states."

One manifestation of the present-day evil that has evoked the "Negro History" Bill, and which illustrates the scope of the required remedy, has been the treatment by historians of the Joint Committee on Reconstruction itself. They have given it, in current parlance, a most unflattering "image." For many decades prior to the rise of the revisionism that was born with the publication of Dr. W. E. B. DuBois' *Black Reconstruction*, it had been the fashion of orthodox (White) American historians to treat the Joint Committee, and particularly the man who conceived it and played a leading role in its work, as vindictive, unfair, and unjust. The name of the man so vilified is Thaddeus Stevens.

It has been traditional for historians to claim that President Andrew Johnson wanted only a just and conciliatory peace with the slave states. The radical opposition to Johnson's "noble and disinterested" peace program, opposition led by Stevens, was said to have been bent on a brutal and vindictive punishment of the South. However, the real truth is that Johnson's peace was a White supremacist's peace, and Stevens sought only to ensure the freedom of Negroes for which so many Whites had fought and died.

One cannot argue here the full case for Thaddeus Stevens, except to suggest that the great weight of evidence, as disclosed and documented in the scholarly published work of the DuBois era, contradicts the negative image that almost all White Americans have been given of this man. Stereotyped as the incarnation of evil in the film *Birth of a Nation* (which merely reflected the Southern school of U. S. history that had by 1911 gained total dominance), Stevens has been consistently so treated in text and popularization ever since. The historical truth is that Stevens spoke for the conscience of America, for brotherhood and decency, and his leadership was indispensable to the embodiment of the Fourteenth Amendment in our Constitution. That Amendment, so little understood by most Americans, was the granite cornerstone that survived the subsequent demolition of the structure of equal rights and federally protected freedom that had been erected by the reconstruction Congress.

What is to the point here, and what almost all scholars who now debate the scope and role of "Black Studies" forget, is the significance of the simple fact that Thaddeus Stevens was not Black. Like John Brown of Harpers Ferry, Stevens was no mere paternalist or philanthropist; he was moved by the perception that no American could be truly free unless all were.

Examples abound of other Whites who served the common cause of justice to Blacks. In a review of Kornbluh's *Rebel Voices* (a documentary history of I. W. W.) in the *Negro History Bulletin*, the writer pointed out that "wobbly" leader "Big Bill" Haywood insisted that his radical labor organization be integrated, and deliberately violated Louisiana's segregation laws in holding meetings of lumberworkers, at the same time that Woodrow Wilson was segregating federal civil service workers.

Dr. John Morsell of the N. A. A. C. P., in the statement prepared for and published in the Hearing of March 18, 1968, pays deserved tribute (p. 34) to a non-political activist whose name and the scope of whose work are unknown to all but a handful of White Americans: Thomas Wentworth Higginson, famed *Colonel of the Black Regiment* and chronicler of his regiment's transition from slavery to manhood in his still neglected masterpiece *Army Life in a Black Regiment.*

V

It should hardly be necessary to argue that it is essential for Whites as well as Blacks to know about such good White men as Stevens, Haywood, and Higginson, to study their lives, careers, and the written records of their thought and work. They have been at best neglected and at worst, especially in such cases as that of Stevens and his contemporary, Massachusetts Senator Charles Sumner, vilified and made the objects of ridicule and contempt. Such character assassination as they suffered was inflicted not so much to defame the dead as for the purpose of degrading the great cause for which they fought. Whites must be instructed that such White men as Sumner and Stevens were giant contributors to the really valuable and rarely published American heritage of brotherhood. Likewise, Blacks who have been repelled by the racism and lawlessness (or the apathy) of much of White America, and driven by it into an extreme form of neo-separatism, need to learn about the good that there has been in the White American past if we are to have any hope for an integrated American future.

Unfortunately, there is the other side to the coin. One is forcibly reminded of it by the publication within the past two years of a new biography extolling the virtues and honoring the memory of President Andrew Johnson. The part played by Johnson in the defeat of a reconstruction based on interracial justice, and thus his guilty complicity in contributing to the giant burden of the present day, is now beyond fair debate. It has been delineated with care in such works as those of the Coxes, McKitrick, Brock and Harold Hyman. Nevertheless the favorable image of the man graven in the hearts and minds of the masters of the White culture structure is well-nigh ineradicable.

The creation and perpetuation of the Andrew Johnson myth was not an act of abstract or antiquarian heroization. Its purpose has been to aid the evil aims to which Johnson contributed by almost every executive and administrative step during his presidency, and such political actions as combating and inciting rejection of the Fourteenth Amendment. The myth must be understood for what it is if we are to shake off the albatross of White racism. A forthcoming study by a long-time student of the Impeachment Trial of 1868 concludes that it is time to come to grips with the proposition that Andrew Johnson deserved to be impeached and that it is a great tragedy that he was not removed.

To enrich the understanding and to quicken the conscience of White Americans, it is insufficient (although necessary) to make them aware that they are heirs to a common tradition that includes such Black geniuses as Douglass and DuBois. But decades of work toward revision of race-relations history will be largely unrewarded if the end-product is narrowed into the channel of belatedly telling only some Blacks that their race had produced great men. Important as that is, it is not enough. Black studies are in danger of falling within the innocuous formulation, "These are the missing pages," used by one consultant in Senate testimony in favor of the Bill. The "missing pages" concept lends itself solely to the name-and-numbers game: a sort of rummaging about for the identity of forgotten inventors, cowboys, and the like. The game succumbs sometimes to the temptation of exaggerating minor achievements, and that can be self-defeating when it goes so far that it is embarrassing to be caught. As Long Island's *Newsday* pointed out, a number of White students who "expressed apathy" toward so-called Black studies courses "said they view them simply as an effort by school administrators to keep Black students quiet."

Therefore, I believe that we need a wholesale revision of that comprehensive judgment upon our past that is embraced in the term "American history." There is nothing that one would ordinarily think of as "Afro-American" about Johnson's impeachment or the role of the I. W. W. in labor history, or the fact that most of the White cofounders of the N. A. A. C. P. were socialist followers of Eugene Victor Debs. What is needed, therefore, is a concept of American studies that will arouse and inform Blacks and Whites alike, that will reach not merely students, but all adults, the mistaught products of an educational system and materials that we now know to have been distorted and viciously unfair to our heritage.

It may be fitting to summarize this discussion, and to introduce the Hearing, with an apt statement from the article "Racism in U. S. History: Unweaving the Threads" by Beatrice Young, Director of Educational Services for the Illinois Commission on Human Relations, and Ben Solomon, Professor at Chicago Teachers' College, published in the Winter/Spring 1968 *Changing Education*, the official publication of the American Federation of Teachers AFL-CIO:

> Afro-American history by itself does not rectify all the White-supremacist distortions of our history. Since White and Black were linked in the system of race relationships, falsification of Black experience must necessarily include falsification of White experience.

The battle for justice to the Negro in our history is but part of the battle for justice to the whole truth in our history.

Howard N. Meyer

CONTENTS

TO ESTABLISH A NATIONAL COMMISSION ON NEGRO HISTORY AND CULTURE

MONDAY, MARCH 18, 1968

House of Representatives,
Select Subcommittee on Labor of the
Committee on Education and Labor,
New York, N.Y.

The subcommittee met at 10:15 a.m., pursuant to notice, in room F, 30 Church Street, New York, N.Y., Hon. James Scheuer, presiding.

Present: Representatives Scheuer, Hathaway, and Hawkins.

Staff members present: Marilyn Myers, clerk; Will Henderson, minority staff; Mrs. Diana Zentay, consultant to the subcommittee.

Mr. Scheuer. The Select Subcommittee on Labor of the House Committee on Education and Labor will come to order. The purpose of our meeting today is to conduct a hearing on H.R. 12962, a bill to provide for the establishment of a Commission on Negro History and Culture.

Without objection, H.R. 12962 will appear in the record at this point.

(H.R. 12962 follows:)

[H.R. 12962, 90th Cong., first sess.]

A BILL To provide for the establishment of a Commission on Negro History and Culture

Be it enacted by the Senate and House of Representatives of the United States of America in Congress assembled, That (a) there is hereby established a Commission to be known as the Commission on Negro History and Culture (hereinafter referred to as the "Commission"). The Commission shall be composed of eleven members, appointed by the President from persons who are authorities on Negro history and culture.

(b) The President shall designate one of the members of the Commission as Chairman, and one as Vice Chairman. Six members of the Commission shall constitute a quorum.

(c) Members of the Commission shall each be entitled to receive $100 per diem when engaged in the performance of the duties vested in the Commission, including traveltime; and while so engaged when away from their home or regular place of business, they may be allowed travel expenses, including per diem in lieu of subsistence, as authorized by section 5703(b) of title 5, United States Code, for persons in Government service employed intermittently.

(d) The Commission shall meet at the call of the Chairman or at the call of a majority of the members thereof.

Sec. 2. (a) The Commission shall have the power to appoint and fix the compensation of such personnel, as it deems advisable, without regard to the provisions of title 5, United States Code, governing appointments in the competitive service, and the provisions of chapter 51 and subchapter III of chapter 53 of such title, relating to classification and General Schedule pay rates.

(b) The Commission may procure, in accordance with the provisions of section 3109 of title 5, United States Code, the temporary or intermitten services of experts or consultants. Persons so employed shall receive compensation at a rate to be fixed by the Commission, but not in excess of $75 per diem, including traveltime. While away from his home or regular place of business in the performance of services for the Commission, any such person may be allowed travel expenses, including per diem in lieu of subsistence, as authorized by section 5703(b) of title 5, United States Code, for persons in the Government service employed intermittently.

SEC. 3. The Commission shall conduct a study of all proposals to create a better understanding and knowledge of Negro history and culture and shall make a recommendation to the President and to the Congress with respect to the legislative enactments which would be necessary to carry out such proposals. Such study shall include consideration of the following:

(1) The steps necessary to unearthing, preserving, and collecting historical materials dealing with Negro history and culture.

(2) What can be done to preserve and catalog existing materials.

(3) Examine the possibilities of the establishment of a Museum of Negro History and Culture or a Center of Negro History and Culture.

(4) Consider where such a museum or center should be located, whether it should be independent or a part of an existing establishment, and how it should be financed.

(5) Consider the methods of disseminating such materials so that the information can be best integrated into the mainstream of American education and life.

SEC. 4. The Commission shall submit a comprehensive report of its findings and recommendations to the President and to the Congress not later than twelve months after the date of enactment of this Act. The Commission shall cease to exist thirty days after such report is submitted.

Mr. SCHEUER. I will only say very briefly before we hear from our distinguished witnesses that the problem of the self image of the Negro person, particularly the Negro child, is one that must concern us all.

Other immigrants to this country such as the Irish, the Poles, the Jews, the Danes, the Italians, you name it, they have their national heroes. They have the consciousness that they have a noble stream of history with a great past, a proud present, and a promising future.

This knowledge that they are a part of something nobler and more enduring than any individual, in effect, gives them a touch of nobility and a touch of greatness too. That is what gives each one of us our self esteem and our identification.

America has not done right by its Negro children. When they go to school and see their primer on "Dick, Jane, and Bow-wow," they have to say, "That is not me," and when they read about the various immigrant groups from Leif Ericson on down to Christopher Columbus, they have to say, "That is not me."

Nowhere in our school books do we portray the magnificent contributions of thousands of Negro Americans to our art, our culture, or our politics. The media today—the press, the radio, the television—also not only fail to portray the distinguished past contributions of the Negro in America, but his present contributions as well.

We must remedy this situation and this oversight, and this gap, and this deficit, and this moral debt that America owes to the Negro in terms of giving him the way to enjoy a self image that is rightfully his. That is why we are here today.

We here have proposed a presidential commission that would study this problem. We can get the true stories of the Negroes of America into the media, into our education system, into the consciousness of every American child, be he Negro or white.

It is also important for the white children to understand that their Negro friends and neighbors have come from a group that has a history, a present, a future, and that they have played a noble role not only in world history, but in American history.

With those very brief remarks, I am happy to welcome my very great friend of many years standing and a distinguished American professor, John Davis.

STATEMENT OF DR. JOHN A. DAVIS, AMERICAN SOCIETY OF AFRICAN CULTURE

Mr. DAVIS. Thank you very much.

Let me say at the outset that I am delighted at the opportunity to speak in support of this bill. I am identified on this statement as a professor and an educator, but I would like to say that I have also been an activist; while fresh out of college I organized the first movement in the United States in 1933. This gives you an idea of my age.

Mr. SCHEUER. I can testify, Professor, to your contributions as an activist in the State commission for human rights. There is no doubt that you have earned those credentials.

Mr. DAVIS. It seems to me that this commission can do three very important things. They are to set the historical record straight, two, to rid white Americans of the stereotypes that have exacerbated race relations in America and, three, to strengthen the self-image of the American Negro, thus improving his capacity and his desire to develop and to compete in our society.

As a byproduct of this work, the commission may well strengthen cultural bridges between America and Africa. With regard to the first objective, for years only the Association for the Study of Negro Life and History, a distinguished organization of Negro historians and a handful of white historians, attempted to reveal the true nature of American history as far as the Negro was concerned.

The first graduate faculty of political science included history and all the social sciences. This was established at Columbia and one would have to say that it took its objectives as a binding up of the wounds of the Nation. In this category one must place such men like Charles Lieber, John Burgess, Dave Muzzey, William Dunning, and Charles Beard, my old professor.

What is important is that these Columbia historians and political scientists came to dominate the textbook field, especially in the secondary schools. Generally, these books presented the Negro Reconstruction leaders as incompetent wastrels; the main motivation of the North in the Civil War as economic rather than moral; Thaddeus Stevens and Charles Sumner were represented as irrational extremists; Lincoln was pictured as a man not committed to abolition but only to saving the Union; and the southerners appeared as justified in their reactions to Reconstruction, although not justified in the terror that they perpetrated.

This approach to American history even infiltrated the history department at Harvard, once dominated by people like Channing and Hart. Not too long ago, about 12 years, if I remember correctly, everyone became aware of a scandal when it was discovered that Morrison and Commager's great textbook, "The Growth of the American Republic," referred to the Negro in the Reconstruction as "Sambo" and said that he was totally unaware and uninvolved in the political struggle that raged. This gives you some idea of how far this process went.

We should not be too hard on these historians and political scientists, for it was the general intent of the power structure in the North and of the opinion-forming institutions that they controlled to rationalize the retreat from Reconstruction to government in the South by the "best people," which usually meant upper class ex-Confederates.

We are indebted to Prof. Rayford Logan for the detailed and scholarly documenting of precisely how the best journals and newspapers in this country rallied to present the Negro as a person for whom no new crusades were justified. In his volume "The Negro in American Mind and Thought: The Nadir, 1877–1901," he shows that once the compromise of 1877 between northern Republicans and southern ex-Confederates was reached in connection with the settlement of the Hayes-Tilden election, most of the great opinion-forming institutions in America turned to the process of accommodating the people of the North to white domination in the South.

This was a dangerous process and let me say that this period, from 1877 to the eighties and nineties when the best families of the South attempted not to take a backward step, was in fact undercaught by opinion. The populous movement resulted in the alliance for whites and Negroes in the South and then the South proceeded to resolve the class problems by racism.

After 1901, no Negro served in Congress until DePriest came from Chicago in 1928, and the South was a bloody bath of terror for the Negro. The man who first analyzed this was, fortunately, a Columbia product, Paul Lewinson, in a volume entitled "Race, Class, and Politics."

In addition to justifying the subordination of Negroes, white historians and social scientists of the past can also be accused of misleading white America by disguising the importance of race in the great political decisions of this country. There has been, therefore, a kind of secret history of the Negro in the United States and of the impact of the race question.

It is for this reason that white America is shocked by the report of the President's National Advisory Commission on Civil Disorder when it says that the underlying cause for such disorders and of the plight of the Negro is white racism. Yet, given a background of 250 years of chattel slavery and 100 years of lynchings and legally enforced discrimination and segregation, what other possible conclusion could be reached?

Fortunately, in recent years, a whole new school of noninterpretive historians who write their history in terms of the record has been concerned with the history of the South and has been setting the record straight. Many of these people are white southerners.

Among these men we can note the works of such men as C. Vann Woodward, Graham, Beale, Cox, and others. They are welcome additions to the historical process.

Should the Commission be established, there will be abundant scholarly research stimulated by such scholars to educate Negro and white Americans about their past. White Americans need to know not only that the shibboleths with regard to the Negro's role in American history are just that, but also that the forebears of northern whites were dedicated and committed to resolving racial problems in America.

The irony is that the southerners have never foresworn those who fought on the side of the Confederacy and that the politicians have pushed the Confederate view. But northerners have been so propagandized in the past that they have foresworn the courageous and dedicated efforts of their forebears.

Negro Americans need to know of their considerable contributions to this country in war and peace, to the accumulation of its wealth, the development of its productivity, to its contributions in medicine, music, and literature, and above all to America's growth in freedom and liberty.

Let me say that one of the ironies of our history is that every time Negroes have moved forward an inch, white America has moved forward 6 or 7 yards. I was on the first Commission of Assistant Director Lehman here in New York and when I started out our first cases were against the U.S. Employment Service. When I returned to the State commission many years later, discrimination against the Jews and against Catholics had all but disappeared, but discrimination against Negroes was still there.

The Commission will also have available to it great new documents, such as the briefs prepared for the Supreme Court's 1954 decision, when the Court asked questions about the historical background of the 14th amendment and the national commitment in this regard, the reports of the President's Civil Rights Commission, and the recent report of the National Advisory Commission on Civil Disorder. The time is ripe and the material is available both in scholarship and in public documents.

With regard to the third objective, ridding America of the stereotypes that have exacerbated race relations in America and to strengthening the self-image of the American Negro, the truthful teaching of history will do a great deal. But there is another area in which much education needs to be done and that is on the subject of race.

The American mind is a veritable grab bag of misconceptions on the subject of race. This can be said of the black man as well as the white, although the racist misconceptions of the white man have been more destructive. There have been notable attempts to educate on this question in the past. One thinks of Gene Weltfish and Ruth Benedict's pamphlet, "The Races of Mankind," and of Herskovits' volume, "Myth of the Negro Past."

There are some more recent publications and some work is being done by those who are interested in intercultural education. But none of this work reflects the degree of professional knowledge and the professional literature in the fields of physical, cultural, and social anthropology, genetics, psychology, psychiatry, and medicine. There is more useful knowledge available now than ever before. One thinks of the work of people like Carlton Coons, and Harris, and Meade, and people like Hogden and others.

The same can be said with regard to historians of the Negro past, especially in Africa. There are people like George Sheppardson and Basil Davidson.

There is, therefore, a great opportunity for the proposed Commission to publish the work in these various fields on a level that can be understood by all Americans. By this process, it can hope to rid America of the vulgar concepts of race. It has often been noted that the

Negro lives in a culture where white is brilliant, white is efficient, white is right, white is powerful, white is rich, white is knowledgeable—and the Negro is nothing.

Certainly, the psychological handicap that the poor Negro American lives under is enough to cripple his ego so that he is unable to martial the energies and confidence necessary to compete and develop. This should suggest to the Commission a highly desirable target; that is to say, the revelation to America and to the American Negro of his contributions to this society.

In this respect the Commission has available to it the work of the Association for the Study of Negro Life and History, the departments of African history in American universities, and the Frederick Douglass Institute and the Museum of Negro Art.

Negroes in white America need to know that they live in a culture that is in part Negro. This is a different point. For years we have been taught that the African came to this country a savage, without culture, and that it has been the problem of America to civilize him. This, of course, is not reality. The Negro was brought here with a culture that enabled him to survive the destructiveness of chattel slavery and that, coupled with his experience in America, has had a profound influence on American culture.

What the white American needs to know is that, in part, he is Negro; that is to say, his culture is in large part Negro. The American's music, dance, humor, speech, food, even his manner of walking, have all been influenced by the Negro. While the southern white man may well have been nurtured by a Negro woman, practically all American children at one time were brought up on African folk tales. These are African folk tales as adapted by American Negroes and white American writers.

These factors are also of profound importance to the American Negro, for although he may be outraged by the American society and alienated against it because it excludes him and discriminates against him, he is not in an alien culture but in one that is in part his own. He needs to know this. His music pours from our radios and his dances have dominated American dance from the cakewalk, the Charleston and the black bottom, through the Lindy hop to the watusi, the slop, and the Broadway.

Americans no longer dance like Europeans, no longer hold women in their arms; they dance separately, as Africans dance, although they dance as partners. What is speech in the Negro ghetto today is the colloquialism for all America tomorrow. Thus, for example, the many uses of the word "cool."

I came down on the subway and I saw that the Citizens Union was advertising for support here in New York. That is what we call a good government organization. They said, "Support the Citizens Union, send us some bread." As I said, this is a distinguished good government organization in New York.

African art was lost in this country because of the disapproval of the masters and the preachers. It had a profound effect upon the greatest of modern artists and through them has influenced the way that all Americans perceive their environment. American Negro youth needs to know African art and its influence on world art. The Negro needs to know what is his in America and white America needs to know, too.

White America enjoys Negro culture. Once it understands this it cannot but orient positively toward the Negro. On the other hand, the Negro's sense of isolation and his sense of alienation will be considerably reduced once he understands that a great deal of what makes life exuberant and enjoyable in America is a result of his contribution.

In terms of what I have been saying, Mr. Chairman, I would like to submit for the record a reprint of an article that I published in The Annals of the American Academy of Political and Social Science entitled "The Influence of Africans on American Culture."

Mr. SCHEUER. Without objection, that article will be printed at the end of your testimony.

Mr. DAVIS. Finally, Mr. Chairman, your proposed Commission's work will supplement work done for years by the American Society of African Culture. I was one of the founders of this organization in 1956 as a result of a conference called in Paris by the leaders of the soon-to-emerge French West African nations. They did emerge as independent nations in 1960.

As a result of that conference, a Society of African Culture, comparable to the Society of European Culture, already in existence, was formed. Their purpose remained investigation, study, and celebration of the contributions of Negro culture—music, art, dance, and literature—not only in Africa but everywhere the Negro has gone: the United States, Cuba, Venezuela, and the islands of the Caribbean.

Both of these organizations have broadened their interests to include a concern with the economic, political, and social developments of the Negro in Africa and the nations of the Western hemisphere. It seems to me, Mr. Chairman, that the work of AMSAC has provided a bridge of understanding between Negro intellectuals and creative persons in Africa and in the Western hemisphere who are mutually interested in the problems of society and the creative contributions of the Negro.

With regard to the latter, the Mãrtiniquan poet, former mayor of Port-au-Prince, and deputy of the French National Assembly, Aime Cesaire, created the word "la negritude," which has been greatly elaborated on by the scholar, poet, and anthologist, Dr. Leopold Sedar Senghor, President of the Republic of Senegal.

These men have noted the fundamental traits of Negro poetry, music, dance, and art wherever the Negro has gone. It is interesting to note that they attribute their first interest in this area to the works of American Negro poets, poetry concerned with protest against caste and race, with the assertion of the validity and humanity of the black man.

It was from the poets of the United States, notably Langston Hughes, Claude McKay, Countee Cullen, Jean Toomer, Melvin Tolson, and Sterling Brown, that West Africans learned to assert the validity of their own culture against the crushing embrace of European culture.

In summary it can be said that Africans are concerned with the same things that American Negroes are concerned with: their contributions to the high culture of the world and the development of their societies.

AMSAC has had two purposes in its work: first, to inform the American Negro of the contributions of his people to American and to world culture and, second, to provide a means by which American Negroes could relate to Negroes elsewhere in the world concerned with the same objectives.

It is unfortunate that AMSAC never had the resources or the organization to reach the black masses of America. If this had been the case, perhaps some of the social confusions of today could have been avoided.

America struggles with the sometimes abrasive nature of black nationalism in this country; but the black nationalist reflects the need of the Negro to know who he is and his own worth. He reflects the problems facing the Negro poor as they develop and become part of the total American society, sharing in its affluence and receiving the rewards offered by the opportunities of social mobility.

What the black nationalist saw in this relationship was unfortunately two negatives and it would have been much better had he incorporated the aspects of the Africans who view their celebration of their culture basically as a means of joining a world culture, of asserting their contributions and their validity in the total society. The purpose is not negative but positive. It is not separation. Its purpose is integration.

I am not proposing that the purpose of this Commission would have anything to do with these international aspects, but I do mean to suggest that one of the results of the Commission's activity would inevitably be to link America's intellectuals and artists, through the literature, with such persons throughout the world.

That is all I have to say, Mr. Chairman. I wish you well in your committee. I hope that your bill is successful.

Mr. SCHEUER. I am very grateful for your testimony, Mr. Davis. I have two distinguished colleagues with me here, Congressman Gus Hawkins of California and Bill Hathaway of Maine. I would like to ask either of them if they would like to respond to your remarks and possibly to ask you some questions.

Mr. HAWKINS. I think my remarks will be in the form of questions rather than a response. I must say, Mr. Davis, that I think your statements are very pertinent and helpful to the committee and that they certainly place the proposal in its proper perspective.

I have had some communications somewhat in opposition to the idea, not to the basic idea, but some of the ramifications of sponsoring or creating a commission to deal specifically with this one subject.

May I try to analyze those comments and seek some comment from you on several things that I think relate to some of these not outright oppositions but some of the reservations.

One, do you believe that such a commission should consist of all Negro, all whites, or what type of a balanced committee or commission do you think would best develop the objectives?

Mr. DAVIS. I think it should be balanced both in terms of race and sections. One of the things that I indicated at the present time is that the field of history now has many white historians who are reevaluating the whole history of the Negro in the United States and especially the history of the South.

It seems to me that it should not be an all-Negro commission.

Mr. HAWKINS. Do you think the purposes of the Commission can only be achieved by Negroes themselves or do you think that the purposes can best be achieved by a balanced commission consisting of various groups?

Mr. DAVIS. I think its purpose can better be achieved by a balanced commission. I don't mean to say by that, that in this area there are not enough Negro skills. There are enough in this area to do the job.

It seems to me that you aren't interested in rewriting Negro history but in getting American history straight. If it is going to be accepted, it should be done with the cooperation of the best scholars in the field.

Mr. SCHEUER. On that point, do you think that in addition to having experts in specifically Negro contributions to history, art, culture, politics, and the like, it might be advisable to have on this Commission some members who are experts in the media, radio, television, the textbook industry, and the like, so that their expertise could contribute to the goal of getting a broad diffusion of this information in our school textbooks and in our information media.

Mr. DAVIS. I think certainly that is so because the job is basically one of communication and education. The field which includes textbooks is a most important field. It has our best illustrators and our best writers and it is a booming industry in the United States.

It is important for children to learn at the outset the nature of their society. If I can refer to some experience in this regard to give you some measure of the problem, it is not my experience but it is my wife's experience.

She came back from Africa once with me and she brought a series of wooden dolls. They were beautifully dressed and handsome people. She came to class and left them home. She was in elementary school and she said, "Next time I want to bring you some dolls just to show you what these people are like. They are very beautiful." A child in the front row said, "Ugh!" She said, "What is wrong with you?" The child said, "If she is black, she can't be beautiful."

Mr. SCHEUER. Is this a Negro child?

Mr. DAVIS. Of course. As sophisticated as my wife is in this field, this was quite a body blow and quite a shock. This is the kind of thing you run up against.

Mr. HAWKINS. One other question, Mr. Davis.

Obviously most of us who have any relationship at all to slum ghettos today are vitally concerned with jobs and other bread and butter issues. There are some who raise the point that instead of going off on what they consider to be a tangent, that is the study of culture and history, that we had better be spending our time talking about how to create jobs and doing something about slum-ghetto problems.

What relationship do you see in this subject and the more economic aspects of creating better job opportunities or better housing or improving the conditions of Negroes? Are we actually going off on a tangent that takes us away from the basic issues and main issues of today in the midst of what might be construed as a social revolution?

What would be your comments on such a position?

Mr. DAVIS. I think they are part of the same thing. Let me say first that one is not a substitute for the other in any way, shape, or form. The question of jobs for able-bodied people—Negro youth without considerable skills or without really any skills in the modern sense—is absolutely necessary and must be done immediately and it must be done on a mass basis.

Automation has just about destroyed everything that those of us in World War II achieved. This was the great movement of Negroes in the industry. We have a generation of young men standing around on corners. We need their work. All you have to do is look at our streets and cities and look at our buildings and you know that we need them. That is an absolute must.

There is also, of course, considerable social disorganization in the Negro community especially with regard to the Negro structure, or lack of it, which must be attacked. These are absolute musts. This is part of the same thing.

As you say, you cannot motivate people to move, to act, and to relate to the total society and to be aggressive intelligently as opposed to being simply destructive unless they believe in somebody, unless their own self-image is important to them and unless they believe they have something to contribute to the society.

What we are experiencing is absolute rage and alienation of the Negro in the society. It seems to me that this Commission would serve a very important function in this regard.

Mr. HAWKINS. Thank you, Mr. Davis.

Mr. SCHEUER. Next is my distinguished colleague from the State of Maine, Congressman William Hathaway.

Mr. HATHAWAY. Thank you, Mr. Chairman.

Thank you, Mr. Davis, for your very enlightening statement.

Let me ask you first of all since our overall objective is to reduce prejudice, do you think that the objective as cited in this bill is going to help to do that? I presume you are going to say "yes" to that. Also, do you have any examples of where it may have worked in other countries?

I am under the impression that in Soviet Russia there is as much prejudice toward the Negroes as there is in the United States. Has a reduction of prejudice been brought about there because of an awareness of the Negro culture or some other reasons?

Mr. DAVIS. The society of African culture was formed in part as an answer to the society of European culture. I don't think that Americans are alone in this business of prejudice.

Mr. HATHAWAY. There are countries with a much lesser degree of it.

Mr. DAVIS. They haven't had the same problem. The British are now facing immigration of Indians and West Indians and their reactions have not been too different from ours. They have a bureau to work on it and they have a bill to legislate on that. I don't know whether it has gone through or not.

Mr. SCHEUER. They have done it in a very un-British fashion and they have prohibited subjects of the Crown with a Crown passport from coming to England. That is unprecedented.

Mr. DAVIS. In some parts they came face to face with reality as to how many people you can get into that island.

Mr. SCHEUER. It wasn't a question just of numbers of people. The percentage of the population in England that is nonwhite is infinitesimal. It is not more than a percentage point or two.

Mr. DAVIS. To answer your question, this question of course exists in Russia. The Russians have put a governmental effort on this. They are autonomous republics and they are organized along cultural grounds. The Supreme Soviet is divided into two parts. One is political and the other is cultural. Even despite a great deal of effort, they have had brutality.

Communism did not solve it. There is a great deal of this element in the conquest of China and Russia. It includes color, but perhaps also the fat and the lean. The Japanese have had it, and the Indians have had it. We are dealing with one of the curses of mankind, it seems to me.

Mr. HATHAWAY. Do you think a lesser degree of prejudice is due to a lesser number of nonwhites and not to an awareness of the cultural background?

Mr. DAVIS. Lesser numbers and because they had imperial responsibilities. These were people who some day were going to grow up and who formed part of their structure. But they lived in foreign lands and had their own countries so one had a different attitude toward them.

The French, for example, right from the beginning were aware of African culture and set out to celebrate it and to incorporate it and to frenchify it in part. It is a different kind of situation.

Mr. HATHAWAY. Can this be a wasted effort? Is there any evidence to show that because more people know about Italian culture there is any less prejudice between non-Italians and Italians?

Mr. DAVIS. There is a difference. You always have a certain question of ethnic adjustments and intergroup friction but it is a different order, it seems to me. You still have friction between the French Canadians and the Anglo-Canadians.

It is quite a different thing from racism in America. Other countries have worked on it. They work on it very much in this fashion. The whole approach to resolving the Canadian friction is cultural, bilingual, and the celebration of French. The stepping up of French universities in Canada, the whole thing to make the French Canadians and all Canadians respect Canada—they do these things in many governmental structures.

Mr. HATHAWAY. Do you think that respect for each other's culture has helped ease the tensions?

Mr. DAVIS. I think so.

What the French Canadians are saying is that it has not been lived up to. Bilingualism exists only in Quebec. This is what they have been demanding. They have also objected to economics. They have commissions for this.

Mr. HATHAWAY. What efforts are being made today to disseminate some information with respect to Negro cultures in various school texts?

Mr. DAVIS. I think John W. Davis can answer that better than I. He has been involved in it. But the publishing companies are aware of this and they are beginning to work on this, especially those who publish for children's books.

The State of California has recently adopted a new book in American history written by two white historians and one Negro historian in an attempt to set it right. Congressman Hawkins will know about that. They are faced with considerable conflicts in this matter as to whether you write a book in the North and you lose a market in the South.

Mr. HATHAWAY. I think you came close to hitting the nail on the head on page 6 when you say that what the white American ought to know is that in part he is Negro. You ought to have a period there.

Mr. DAVIS. The etymological data is that mankind developed in Africa and moved. There are a lot of geneticists who substantiate this. There is a lot of information which substantiates this.

Mr. HATHAWAY. It would be more striking if it were known and appreciated.

Mr. DAVIS. Yes.

Mr. HATHAWAY. Thank you.

Mr. SCHEUER. Thank you very much for your courtesy in coming here and giving us this very interesting and stimulating testimony.

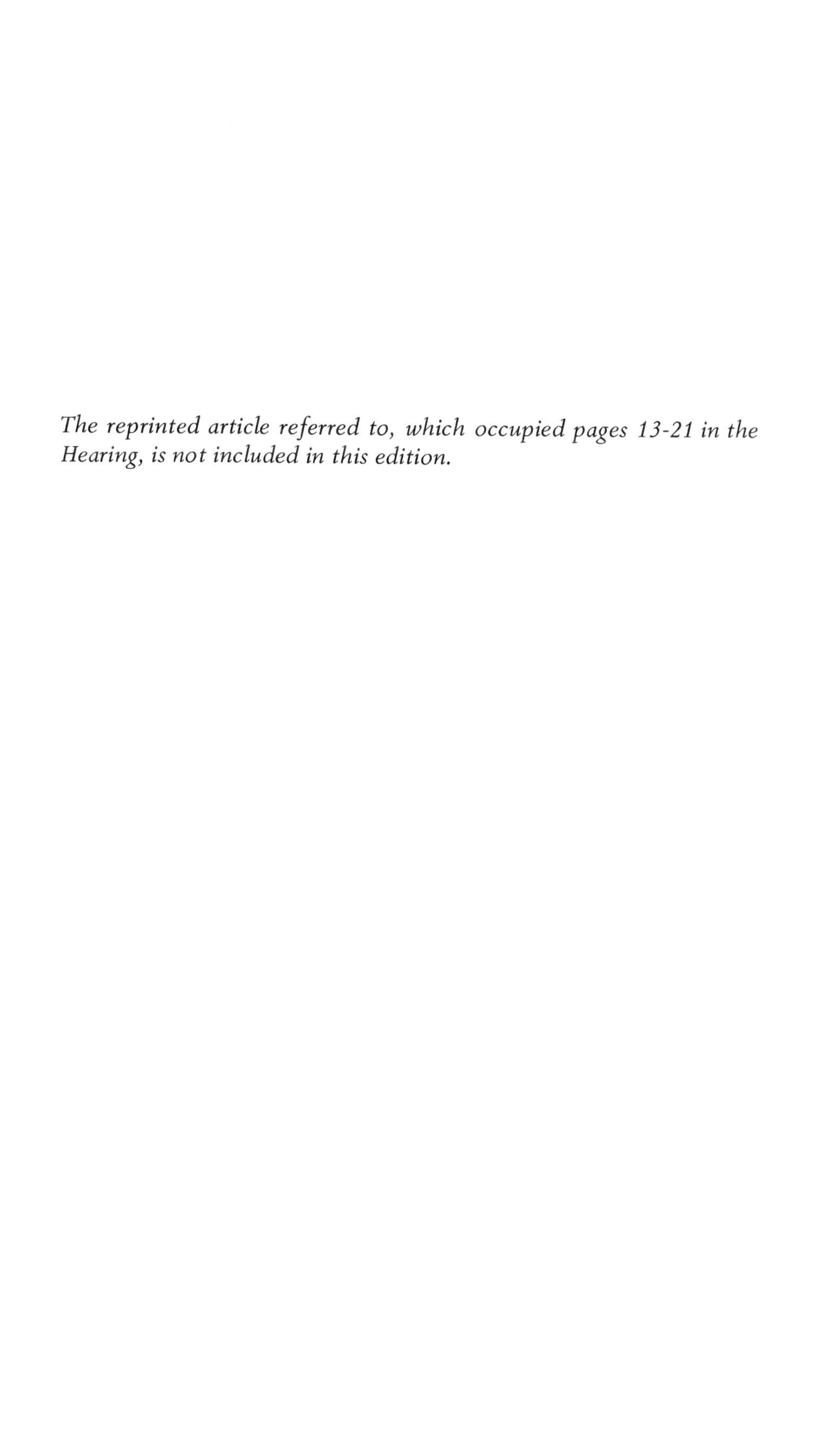

The reprinted article referred to, which occupied pages 13-21 in the Hearing, is not included in this edition.

Mr. SCHEUER. Our next witness is Mr. Roy Innis.
Please go ahead, Mr. Innis.

STATEMENT OF ROY INNIS, CORE

Mr. INNIS. I am the associate national director of CORE. For the record, I am also a black nationalist.

I think we should start by discussing what I consider the relevance of this Commission. There is no doubt that it is not going to directly cure or contribute tremendously to many of the ills of the ghetto at this time, but I think it would be shortsighted of us if we do not see the importance of dealing with this problem in a complete fashion. In other words, it must be a unity of the sociological, socioeconomic, and sociopolitical solutions to the problem.

I consider this under sociopsychological. I think in that vein we should start off, first of all, with the name of the Commission. It is no secret in these days that black people in this country are moving away from the name Negro to that of black or African American.

I would think that it would be fitting of this committee and it would be a start in the right direction if we would take this into consideration and instead of referring to the Commission as Negro History and Culture, refer to it as either the Commission of Black History and Culture or African-American History and Culture.

I don't think it would help to clarify the objectives if you say you have a Commission on Negro History and Culture. I don't know what you are talking about. I don't know whether you are talking about the history of black people in this country or the history of black people all over the world.

Mr. SCHEUER. I think it would be both of those things.

Mr. INNIS. You are talking about the history of African America?

Mr. SCHEUER. We are talking about the black republics of Africa.

Mr. INNIS. You are talking about the history of black people. The other point, as to who shall appoint this committee, again I feel we must recognize the credibility gap that exists between blacks and whites in this country. I think we should be more and more realistic in light of the impending catastrophe that is about to occur between black and white. We should not kid ourselves about our relationships.

The Commission will have a great deal more credibility if it is not appointed by the President, but by a conference of black leadership. They shall compose a committee. I differ with the previous speaker who suggested that the committee should be composed of blacks and whites. It is a study of the history of black people.

Mr. SCHEUER. Let me just correct you there. It is more than just a study of the history of black people. It is a study of the history of black people, their contributions to our culture and history, the development of a culture in Africa, in art and literature, the development of national states in Africa and, very importantly, how the story of this great contribution to world art, history, culture, politics, and literature can be disseminated in our education system and in our media.

It is not only the compilation and the study of the contributions themselves, but just as important, the study and the development of programs for the broad-scale dissemination of this information.

Mr. INNIS. I would suggest that you have in fact made my point even more. It is for that reason, especially, that I would want to see this Commission composed of the people who are most affected by this problem, black people.

I think we should move forward wherever possible, and in this case it is possible. We do have eminent scholars in this area and if we did not have eminent scholars, I would call on anybody else, whites or Chinese.

Since we do have our scholars and since the problem deals with us and since we are the ones who suffer most, I would want to see the Commission composed of black people. They should be eminent black scholars selected by a conference of black leadership.

As to what should be studied, you have described quite adequately many of the things that I want to point out. I think what would be very important in addition to the study of the African background and the Afro-American, is to study the early sociopolitical philosophy taught by the early nationalists.

I think we have a situation in America wherein whenever you talk about black social thought, we almost always refer to the Frederick Douglasses, the DuBois', and such. Very little attention is paid to the great nationalist philosophers—the Ed Blightens, the Martin Delaneys.

These are men who were proposing solutions to the impending catastrophe that we face now way back in the time of slavery. I think an adequate study of this is important, bringing these men to the height and recognition that they so deserve. We should point out the relevance of much of their solutions.

Much of the direction that we are moving in now, both blacks and whites, is very much based on many of the problems that these men suggested.

I think, again, whenever we are dealing with the problems of black people in America in any way, we should keep in mind the need for the creation of indigenous institutions, black institutions, institutions of our own.

I think it serves no function to have this Commission to serve for 1 year and then drop out of existence. I think it is important that if this Commission is going to serve a function it must exist longer than 1 year.

I am uncertain that the history of black people and the culture of black people can be studied in 1 year. I would want to see it transferred into an institute for black history and culture.

Mr. SCHEUER. May I say this. You are exactly on point. This Commission is not going to do a study or a compilation itself. It is going to recommend to the Congress and to the President what agencies or institutions or commissions or institutes should be established for this.

You are quite right in saying that it is ridiculous to think that any kind of scholarly job could be done in a year. This process if done right will probably take 5 years or 10 years. What this Commission would do is to evaluate the broad-scale problem and then recommend the funding, the institutions, the systems, and the devices that must be used and to compile the existing data and to disseminate it.

This Commission is not going to do the work itself. It is going to survey the field and come up with a broad-scale program of the work to be done and the door of our media that ought to be opened. It couldn't possibly be done in a year. That is not our intent.

Mr. INNIS. The point I want to emphasize is that here, as in any other endeavor dealing with black-white relationships, we should always move to the creation of black institutions. We need to have instruments through which we can attempt to satisfy our needs. We need an unborn institute to deal with the study. To deal with this area of black existence could be of great contribution to both of the peoples living in this country.

I must say that it is important that this Commission recognizes that we are two people and not lull themselves into the dreamland of one nation. I think we must recognize some of the findings of the Commission, the Civil Disorder Commission, that spoke of moving towards a two-society nation.

I think we probably want to correct that slightly. We have always been, throughout existence, a two-society nation. We must recognize this and we must rectify the inequities between them. Basically this is the material that I wanted to give to this committee.

Thank you.

Mr. SCHEUER. I am going to call on my colleague, Gus Hawkins, from California first and then Mr. Hathaway and then I will have a few questions.

Mr. HAWKINS. Mr. Innis, you are also an officer with the Harlem Commonwealth Council Committee. At this time I would like to thank you—it is off the subject, I know—for the interesting meeting which I attended and the courtesy which you showed me and my associates when we visited your committee hearing and I certainly want to commend you on the manner in which it was being approached. I hope that the invitation which I extended to you at that time of continuing some dialog with your group so that there would be some relationship between my own area in Los Angeles and yours still stands. I certainly would appreciate hearing from you.

There are some things that I disagree with and some things that I agree with in what you have said. Your views are slightly different than mine in terms of the widening gap between the two groups in America. I differ completely with that.

However, I do respect the reasons why you have concluded that that is desirable; however, I am more inclined to believe as the previous witness has said, that in a sense we are one people in background. If this Commission, it seems to me, achieves anything, it will be to show the common background of people and it is because of that, what I consider to be scientific fact, that I cannot accept the other conclusion.

I would like for you to elaborate on this in terms of this feeling on which I constructively disagree with you.

Mr. INNIS. I think we disagree semantically. I think you assume from my statement that for people to operate separately is to widen the gap. I submit this is not true at all. I will submit that people never lived so closely as the slave and his master in the plantation. They lived so close that black women used to nurse white babies.

The fact is that the physical closeness is not closeness at all in a sociological sense. The status relationship between two people is what makes them close. Canadians and Americans have more social intercourse than black and white Americans living in the same city. Why? Is it because of physical closeness? No. It is because of the status.

For us to move towards black institutions is in fact to narrow the gap. It is in fact to make it easy for white Americans to adequately and accurately judge white people. They cannot do this now and this cannot come through mixed commissions. It did not come through mixed institutions or so-called institutions. It will come only when whites can see grandeur, glory, and status in black institutions.

Mr. HAWKINS. I am glad you did elaborate on it. It certainly reduces somewhat the differences in our opinions. Do you believe that since whites are the ones who distorted history, that they had a leading role and responsibility actually for creating it, and for that reason should be asked to serve in a leadership and a constructive role in correcting that which they actually created? That they should correct the injustices which they rendered in history?

Mr. INNIS. Let me say that it is exactly for that reason that I wouldn't want them to correct it.

Mr. HAWKINS. I meant in terms of serving on commissions and taking an active role in this.

Mr. INNIS. The black social thought and black history as written now is written by whites and they already have had a chance. They have the media available to them and the publishing industry.

We did not have an equal chance to write our own history. We need this chance. Secondly, if we have to go by the Civil Disorder Report, they say that the problem in America is a problem of white racism. But the Commission did not go deeply enough into a definition of racism.

Let me try for a brief moment to describe it. There is racism of the individual nature, the obvious ones, the "Bull" Connor-type racism and there is even a more dangerous one; there is an institutional racism.

This racism makes every American child a racist almost from birth without having a choice in the matter. My wife, who is a supervisor in a publishing firm, had an experience wherein one of the girls who worked for her, a white girl—she has all white workers—who brought her baby to work.

The baby did not go to any of the white workers. The baby went to my wife. Why? Was it because the baby loved white people, because the baby knew my wife was the supervisor? No. The baby thought my wife was the nurse. She thought she was the maid. The baby is a racist.

Obviously, we do not mean to penalize a baby. We are not blaming that baby for any crime, but we must recognize a fact that the baby doesn't have a chance. The baby is growing up in an environment and is going to internalize certain values and they are going to cause that baby to make negative judgments of me whether the baby wants to or not.

For that reason, we must be careful when we are writing vital things about a people's history and culture. Let us face it, history is a record of a people of itself. Black people must have that right like all healthy human beings any time in the history of mankind.

We have been denied that opportunity because of recent past history. There is a time for us now to rectify this. You must have confidence in our scholars. You must assume that they will do an adequate and objective job. I will submit that they are better able because the effects of institutional racism might be less on them. If history must lie, at least let it lie on your side.

Mr. HAWKINS. Just one final question. You referred to the appointment of this Commission not by the President but by, I think you referred to a conference. Would you elaborate on that procedure which I suggested.

Mr. INNIS. Yes, I think black people have more at stake and that a credibility gap exists between blacks and whites. I keep pressing this but not to widen the gap any more. I don't think it can be widened any more. I think it has been stretched to the limits already. I think we must accurately analyze the problem.

Mr. HAWKINS. What I referred to, to be a little more specific, was—if the President doesn't actually hold a conference of whoever is going to be there and select the person who is going to do this work, in other words, if you are going to have a conference of black people, who is going to issue the call and who is going to do this?

Mr. INNIS. The President can convene a meeting of black leadership across the country. I think this was done a couple of years ago. A general conference on civil rights, I think it was called. He can convene the conference and once it is convened we then take over and organize ourselves.

Mr. HAWKINS. You are suggesting that the President should convene a conference and that the conference would consist only of black people, is that it?

Mr. INNIS. Yes, black leadership across the country.

Mr. HAWKINS. This conference itself should be the one to select the members of a commission?

Mr. INNIS. Right.

Mr. HAWKINS. Who in turn would carry out the objectives of this idea?

Mr. INNIS. Right. This would tend to make an institution that is ours. Other people came to this country and brought with them their own institutions. Black people when they were brought to this country had all of their institutions removed. It is for this reason that we should always attempt to replace them. We should always attempt to turn over public institutions that are dealing with black people to blacks and to be managed by blacks. Institutions create values and they regulate behavior.

Mr. HAWKINS. Thank you.

Mr. SCHEUER. Mr. Hathaway.

Mr. HATHAWAY. Thank you very much, Mr. Innis, for your testimony.

I don't quite understand why you want blacks only on the Commission. Is it just because you feel that blacks have more expertise or do you think the Commission should be solely black regardless of whether the expertise lies in any particular nationality?

Mr. INNIS. I stated that if we did not have our own scholars then I will use Chinese or white scholars. I feel that we do have our own eminent scholars. For this reason we should use them.

Mr. HATHAWAY. Is there an outstanding Chinese scholar in this field?

Mr. INNIS. I am certain that a black leadership conference would be pragmatic and select that individual.

Mr. HATHAWAY. It might not be composed of black only.

Mr. INNIS. I would prefer it to be composed of blacks since you are writing the history of blacks. As I stated, there is no close-off of whites writing about black history. They have been writing about black history for centuries and they will continue. They have all the medias available for doing it.

The other reason I gave is because of the racist nature of America and the nature of racism that so permeates every single institution and individual in America and that there is less danger of racism being an influencing factor in this Commission if it is all black.

Mr. HATHAWAY. But as a practical matter, since the report of the Commission would come back to the Congress for some kind of action——

Mr. INNIS. They should have the purest possible document to deal from.

Mr. HATHAWAY. But as a practical matter, since the report of the Congressmen, wouldn't they be more objective if we had a spread of different races on the Commission?

Mr. INNIS. I will hope that the Congress will look at the report objectively and look at the material developed and the compelling logic of their conclusions. I hope that will be the influencing factor. If you are going to use other factors they would be used whether you had three white liberals on the committee or not.

Mr. HATHAWAY. Do you think that there would be some hope with mixed members that that would reduce the prejudice barrier?

Mr. INNIS. I think it would help to rectify certain mistaken notions in the minds of many Americans, black and white. I think there is no secret that black people suffer equally or not quite equally, but to a great extent, from the effects of racism in that they too make very negative judgments of blacks.

I think the previous speaker spoke of a black girl who was shocked to hear the word black used with beautiful. We too suffer from this effect. This will help us and will also help whites in making judgments of blacks.

Mr. HATHAWAY. Is there any evidence of this in any other society?

Mr. INNIS. I think the evidence is that in every society history and culture is an extremely vital thing and that those people themselves make certain that their young get from the cradle to the grave. We can see the nature of an American curriculum which is full of American history and culture from the first grade to college.

It is always the attempt of any society toward the history of mankind to deal with its young through its culture in history from their points of view and from its lips. That is the important thing. All people throughout history, I suspect from the caveman days, will give history to the young from their own lips.

This has been denied black people and dispels some of the problems we have in terms of achievements of black people. This is the inability to relate themselves back to anything else.

Mr. HATHAWAY. You are talking about black people everywhere.

Mr. INNIS. This effects black people everywhere, but mostly those in the United States who are under Anglo-Saxon domination.

Mr. HATHAWAY. Is there any evidence of a country like France or Italy in which the knowledge of the cultural background of black people has helped these racial tensions?

Mr. INNIS. I don't think that the same kind of racial tension exists in Italy or France that we have here in this country. I think that it would be inaccurate to suggest that the racism that we have here is even equivalent to that in Britain, even with their present crisis.

We have a unique phenomenon. I think this country has been an innovator in the dealing of man to man. I think the nature of the slavery developing in this country, and slavery is a very old institution, the nature of this one is a unique thing to mankind.

It is no longer as it was in the past, an unfortunate economic state of being for a slave. For the oppressed in this country were subject to something much more insidious, something much more debilitating to the oppressed.

Mr. SCHEUER. In what way?

Mr. INNIS. In that while slavery was very cruel physically to the body of the individual, the American brand was cruel to the individual. Even though this will kill the body, the Americans kill the mind. The body remained and you create a hybrid class, a class of zombies. You create people with no language, people with no values of their own, people with no myth, no God of their own. All the vital ingredients for being a man are missing.

My heroes as a kid were Andy Jackson and George Washington. They might be great cats but I would prefer to have more heroes that I can see myself in. This cannot be done for blacks. I think if we go in the ghetto and take any 10 black kids at random and ask for a list of their heros, I think you will find nine of them will say George Washingtons, Andy Jacksons, and Jack Kennedys. I think we must see there is something unhealthy about this.

Mr. HATHAWAY. Do you say the slave aspect has made the people in the United States more prejudiced than in other countries?

Mr. INNIS. Yes. I refer to the nature of the slavery and the nature of the relationship between blacks and whites.

Mr. HATHAWAY. We have had a history of other nations of whites enslaving other whites, and yet the prejudice did not come about as it has come here.

Mr. INNIS. That is because these other people define slavery quite differently from the American. The slave was not a subhuman.

Mr. HATHAWAY. The Roman slave was more oppressed.

Mr. INNIS. But better respected. A Greek slave in Rome was respected. He was not considered subhuman at all. At times he must have been considered a bit brighter. He was a teacher of the Roman so obviously there is quite a different concept of slavery. The dehumanizing aspect of American slavery didn't exist anywhere else in the world.

Mr. HATHAWAY. Thank you very much.

Mr. SCHEUER. Mr. Innis, we have enjoyed your testimony very, very much and I think we are all in your debt. You have certainly told it like it is. While some of us may have some differences of opinion with some of your conclusions, you have certainly laid it on the line and given us some very powerful truths and for that we are grateful.

You mentioned this white child who you have accurately described as having been developed at a very early age by our institutions. Perhaps not a bigot, she certainly accrued manners of thought reaction that will not help that child respect the broad variety of Americans as being equals.

Don't you think that that child has suffered from what you characterized as being turned into a bigot at a very early age?

Mr. INNIS. Of course, I sympathize with that child and myself because I suffer from that child.

Mr. SCHEUER. You think the child has suffered.

Mr. INNIS. Yes.

Mr. SCHEUER. Don't you think there is a real interest on the part of the 190 million Americans in rooting out the institutions of bigotry in our society?

Mr. INNIS. If that was so, it is all the more reason why I will then say to those Americans, "Let me help you to uproot this poison that was placed in you unconsciously." The way to help you is not to have you join me in the creation of my values and the recording of my history and tracing of my culture but to help me present it to you after I have done it and for you to present yourself to me after you have done it.

I will suspect that there is more understanding between nations with different cultures and language than you have between whites and blacks in America. It seems to me that people doing things separately or apart is not a criteria itself for creating a gulf between them.

The understanding, the ability to make adequate judgments, is needed. White people cannot make positive judgments of blacks. Why? Because they use white values to do it. White values were created for white people as it should be. It is up to me now to create black values to help you to judge me.

Mr. SCHEUER. Let us put it this way. These institutions that you talked about were basically created by a predominently white society.

Mr. INNIS. Yes, based on white values.

Mr. SCHEUER. And white children as well as white adults have suffered from the fact that these institutions came about.

Mr. INNIS. Let us clarify the meaning of the word suffer. Clearly there are those who tell me that slavery was a brutal institution and

94-721 O—68——3

that the slave master suffered psychological damage as did the slave; of course, I can agree with this in a kind of esoteric sense. If we had a choice, however, we would switch roles.

The suffering is quite different. The white baby has been scarred possibly irreparably. The fact is when that baby is penalizing me as a police chief, as a judge, as a senator, a representative, or any leader of an institution in the American culture, I am going to suffer a lot more than that.

Mr. SCHEUER. No question about it. Let us establish the point that number one, white people who have been formed by these institutions have suffered, as you say, irreparable scars. Number two, the white educational institutions and our media as they are presently run inadequately portray the dignity and the worth, and the contributions of our black citizens. This demeans and impoverishes whites as well as blacks.

Since these institutions were formed and organized and are presently controlled basically by whites, don't you think that white liberals—and I don't know whether you used that as a pejorative phrase or not—not only have a responsibility but perhaps are in a favorable position to exercise their leadership in white society to change these institutions. Don't you think it would be helpful to have whites who are deeply concerned about the failures of their institutions to disseminate the word of the worth and the contributions of our black citizens? Can't they play a positive role along with qualified blacks in arriving at a program together?

Mr. INNIS. I don't see why or how my solution can close off the whites. If we had a black commission, I will suspect that there will be nothing wrong for calling whites for testimony. I suspect that whites would not be inhibited from publishing their own testimony.

I would suspect that after we submit a document to the Congress or the President that white liberals cannot at that time support many of the solutions or the programs offered from this. There is no close off at all.

This is in no way turning away help. The best possible document from the point of view of the black people is to have black people, like all people throughout the history of mankind, do it themselves. Let them create their own history and trace their own culture.

It is no secret that the version of Canadian history dealing with the War of 1812 is quite different from the American version of the same war.

Mr. SCHEUER. You probably also know that the Civil War is described in text books distributed in the North as the Civil War, but the same text book will have a separate edition distributed in the South which call it the War Between the States.

Mr. INNIS. All we are saying then is that people write history from their own eyes and ears and through their own mouths for their young and I am saying that black people have been denied this right.

It might not be the ideal way to arrive at truth but then why should we expect this with blacks only? We have been suffering from not having similar instruments to deal with our particular needs, our cultural needs.

I am saying here that Congress has a good chance to restore the trend to black people. We must not have a segregated institution because we have had those; we must have separate, different institutions. There is a difference. A segregated institution is one that is apart from a white institution but that is run by whites.

That is the nature of all institutions that regulate black people's lives in this country. A separate institution is something similar to your small State and your big State. You have Connecticut with its own institutions, and you have New York with its own institutions, and the both of them join in a partnership in a nation.

Mr. SCHEUER. As I get it, what you and we are concerned about is the fact that white institutions or institutions that are controlled by whites but which service the entire population aren't presenting the kind of a picture we like to present. The great broadcasting networks, the great newspapers of our country, the magazines, the great publishing houses, these are controlled by whites. They are serving a predominently white society. They are presenting an inadequate story of the contributions of blacks to our society and the history of the black republics of Africa and don't we want to change these white institutions to get them to straighten up and fly right?

Isn't it unlikely that you are going to be able to create black television networks and radio stations and black national magazines and newspapers to cover the entire spectrum of the American population and, therefore, isn't the challenge to change the white media and the basically white controlled education system and the basically white textbook publishing industry so that they portray the full story that we have been talking about?

Mr. INNIS. I would say no. I would say that is the least pragmatic way. It has been tried and it failed. I would say that the way to do it is for blacks to create their own objects of excellence and the compelling logic of this will itself force these white institutions to function better and more accurately.

Mr. SCHEUER. We would agree with that a thousand percent.

Mr. INNIS. I don't think that we can really expect to change these white institutions. We must create parallel black institutions, show the excellence in them, and then the white institutions can learn from them.

Mr. SCHEUER. Are you in effect saying that we shouldn't try to work with the television networks and the magazines?

Mr. INNIS. For me to move to a black institution is not that you should try to stop white institutions. It is a continuing battle. I should say that priorities should be established. If I have a limited amount of resources, I will want to put those resources in the creation of black institutions. Black instruments that can in fact be used as instruments for reforming white institutions.

Mr. SCHEUER. What kind of institutions are you discussing?

Mr. INNIS. I am referring to all institutions that relate to any and all aspects of America. We must recognize the failure of the attempt to integrate schools since the Brown decision in 1954. I think statistics that I get and the Government itself will indicate that it is not moving in the right direction.

Mr. SCHEUER. It is moving but painfully and pathetically slow.

Mr. INNIS. I think that the way to deal with improving education of black kids is not to reform white educational institutions but to create black educational institutions. Mind you, I am not suggesting creating segregated institutions. We have them now. I am saying that integrated white institutions are unreal.

Whites are not going to do it and we don't have enough power to make them do it. But we can create black educational institutions. In Harlem they tried to work through the New York City educational system to improve education and Harlem we know has been a failure. They have tried all the magic band aid palliative solutions. You can list about 20 initials for programs they have tried and we know they have failed.

What we are saying now is the cure of this ill is the creation of a Harlem education system. It is not going to be some little hole-in-the-wall system. It is going to be a large system. It is going to be the third largest system in the State and one of the largest ones in the country.

I am saying that this could show the example and act as the guide to future relationship between blacks and whites because if we can have a Harlem education system and we can improve the education of blacks in Harlem, improve matters and turn out better individuals out of our school system, show more progress, show more achievement, the compelling logic of that will indicate that maybe we should control other institutions.

Let us examine this for a while. Suppose Harlem was a white suburban area, would it be so unusual for them to sue for their own institutions? No. In fact, it is the normal pattern in American life. The people of a particular interest group constitute themselves into a political subdivision of a State or Federal Government.

That political subdivision tries to control their own organization giving services to the area. The fact is, services are better when it is done that way. Services in Harlem in education, in sanitation, police protection, health, welfare, you name it, are all poor—vis-a-vis, services in other parts of New York City or other parts of other urban centers.

I am also suggesting the only solution to the impending crisis and the impending catastrophe between blacks and whites is the creation of indigenous black institutions to serve and to be directed by and to regulate the lives of people indigenous to the particular areas.

We have to have black educational institutions. We have to have a black welfare system and black hospitals. Our hospitals are hideous. Other people can get by this because they have their own institutions. They have enough private funds to create their own health centers, their own schools. We don't have that kind of funds.

We pay taxes. Give us a rebate of taxes to run our own institutions and we will better distribute the goods and services in our area.

Mr. HATHAWAY. Going back to a separate and equal——

Mr. INNIS. This was a semantic argument that confused the whole relationship between blacks and whites way back in 1898 with the Philson decision which was a mistake. They didn't understand the language they were using up to the 1954 Brown decision, again another mistake. They don't know the language they are using.

Let us consider three terms, integration, separation, and segregation. The attempt is always made to define these words in strictly geographic terms. Consequently, segregation and separation end up being people living in different geographic areas. That is not the only definition. In fact, it is an inadequate and dangerous definition because by the definition, I will have to assume that New Jersey is segregated from New York and it is not. I will have to assume that Yonkers is separated from New York City, and that Mount Vernon is separated from New York City. It is not true.

They are separate political subdivisions. They are separate from each other in that they control their own institutions. They are not segregated. Segregation is in a heterogeneous culture with these two groups. It is the control of institutions and the flow of goods and services in one area by people in another area. That is segregation.

Whether you are north or south, it is the same thing. In the South, even though people live in the same block, blacks and whites, the institutions are in different places. The bad thing is that they are controlled by the same people. There is no doubt about who controls the southern institutions.

In the North it is the same thing. You have a common institution. But the services given to the black areas is not equitable in terms of the total availability of goods and services. That, too, is segregation because a certain location, a certain group of people with a particular interest, is being governed by someone outside that area.

We must clarify even for the Supreme Court the difference between segregation and separation. Now to go further, to say that segregation is bad, and I agree, is not to say that reality can only be described in terms of integration. Integration is not the contradictory of segregation, it can be the contrary, which means that both can be wrong.

Let us consider integration for a moment. Suppose black people, 86 percent of us, should leave these urban centers and spread ourselves out like licorice on a white cake. In terms of the American democracy we have in this country, how would black people ever, in any political subdivision, be able to reflect their own interests? Isn't it that people in a democracy follow and reflect their interest? Isn't it that there should be protection for minorities?

They organize in smaller and smaller political subdivisions. Would black people be able to institute themselves as a majority in any political subdivision? The answer is no.

Mr. SCHEUER. Let me just ask you this question. Apart from your feeling that the Commission ought to be a black commission and the members ought to be selected by a convention of Afro-American leaders, do you agree with the principles of this Commission apart from that?

Mr. INNIS. Yes, in that there is a need for a definitive study of black history and culture.

Mr. SCHEUER. And that it ought to be disseminated to all Americans?

Mr. INNIS. Right.

Mr. SCHEUER. I want to thank you for your stimulating testimony.

I would like to announce that the distinguished American author James Baldwin has flown in from California. He is going to testify immediately after the next witness who will be Dr. John Morsell. Dr. Morsell is the associate director of the NAACP and we are very happy to have him here this morning.

Dr. Morsell, your testimony will be printed in its entirety at this point in the record. So, perhaps you would like to simply speak off the cuff and tell us of your thoughts.

(The statement of John Morsell follows:)

TESTIMONY OF JOHN MORSELL, ASSISTANT EXECUTIVE DIRECTOR, NATIONAL ASSOCIATION FOR THE ADVANCEMENT OF COLORED PEOPLE, NEW YORK CITY

Chairman Scheuer and Members of the Select Subcommittee, I wish to express appreciation on behalf of the National Association for the Advancement of Colored People for this opportunity to testify on H.R. 12962. Let me say at the outset that my organization heartily endorses the bill and its objectives and that we will lend our fullest support to the efforts that will be made to secure its enactment. May I add a word of deep appreciation to Congressman Scheuer and those who have joined him in the sponsorship of H.R. 12962.

Very possibly the first systematic attention to the problem of exploring and recording the history of the Negro in the United States was undertaken 107 years ago by Thomas Wentworth Higginson. It is not generally known that this was a major interest of Higginson's and in a very illuminating way the fact that he was interested and the circumstances surrounding it have great pertinence for the objectives of the proposed bill.

Thomas Wentworth Higginson—author, lecturer and publicist—was one of the staunchest abolitionists, both in his native Massachusetts and elsewhere. But he was more than a pamphleteer; he was a man of action. During the years of the bloody conflict in the Kansas-Nebraska territory between "free soilers" and pro-slavery men, Higginson journeyed to Kansas to bring arms and other supplies to the embattled anti-slavery settlers. He was a supporter and backer of John Brown and even entertained for a brief while the idea of a rescue mission after Brown's capture at Harper's Ferry.

But the crowning achievement of Higginson's career was his service as colonel of the first all-black regiment recruited into the Union army, made up almost entirely of newly-freed South Carolina slaves. Higginson found that this one simple undertaking encompassed the entire issue of the Negro's worth as a man and his capacity to respond to opportunity. A stirring account of what he and his officers learned and of what both they and their valiant soldiers learned from the experience has been set forth by Higginson in his diary, "Army Life in a Black Regiment," recent republished in paperback.

Higginson's biographical sketches of noteworthy Negro leaders, including Nat Turner, were the forerunners of the concern which ultimately became embodied in the programs of the NAACP and in the formation by Carter G. Woodson of the specialized Association for the Study of Negro Life and History. In the activity of these organizations, the unearthing and the publicizing of the facts regarding the Negro's life, vicissitudes, struggles, failures and successes, first a bondsman, then as an aspiring citizen in this country has been of paramount importance.

Even under ordinary circumstances, this would be a massive undertaking—one which becomes more and more difficult the longer it is deferred, since records are perishable and memories are even more so. But the Negro, peculiarly, in this country has had to contend with something more—namely, a conspiracy on the part of the historical profession to inhibit or distort or minimize the truth regarding the Negro in America. It is only in comparatively recent years that we have begun to witness a shift, with the advent of younger and newer historians, relatively free of racism and bias, who have proceeded to re-write much bad history in the interest of accuracy and honesty. It is not accidental, of course, that many of these newer historians are Negroes who have benefited from access to the tools of learning and who have seen as a principal obligation the righting of the ancient wrongs.

In spite of what has been done, and in spite of the growth of active endeavors in this direction, the areas of ignorance and misconception are still infinitely vaster than the areas of knowledge. By far the bulk of the history textbooks and supporting materials used in the public schools in our country at present are either inadequate or grossly erroneous in their accounts of the Negro's role in the nation's development. The need, therefore, for a commission such as is provided for in H.R. 12962 is quite clear. It is the responsibility of enlightened government to provide the means whereby its citizens can attain the required degree of corresponding enlightenment. Such a commission at the national level is further justified by the obvious fact that the benefits of knowing the truth about Negro history and culture are as great for white Americans as they are for Negro Americans.

It is widely recognized now in the Negro community that the task of building confidence and a sense of worth is sadly impeded if Negro young people are unable to have a general knowledge of their heritage. It is not so thoroughly recognized, however, that the white child who grows up with pride in his heritage as a Jew or as a descendant of Italians, Englishmen, Irishmen or Germans, but who sees Negroes as devoid of such a heritage, is likely to fall ready prey to prejudice and to attributions of inferiority to his Negro fellows.

It is my earnest hope that, after careful consideration of the testimony of witnesses and of what its other investigations will show, the Select Subcommittee will report to the full commitee and work for the adoption, there and in the House of Representatives itself, of legislation embodying the proposals of H.R. 12962.

Thank you very much.

STATEMENT OF JOHN MORSELL, ASSOCIATE EXECUTIVE DIRECTOR, NATIONAL ASSOCIATION FOR THE ADVANCEMENT OF COLORED PEOPLE, NEW YORK CITY

Mr. MORSELL. I first, of course, want to express the appreciation of my organization as well as of myself for the opportunity to testify on H.R. 12962.

I would like to elaborate on the testimony largely in the direction of two issues that appear to have arisen in the questioning of the earlier witnesses.

Congressman Hathaway, for example, was greatly concerned or was interested in knowing whether there were any counterparts in other countries of this kind of action, whether there was any evidence to show, for example, in France or Spain or Italy or wherever, that the widespread knowledge and dissemination of the histories of a minority improved the relationships.

Of course, as both witnesses indicated and as Congresssman Hathaway certainly knows, there is no counterpart in the first place to the American racial history. There are, however—and I think perhaps the state of Israel presents the best illustration in modern times—cases in which nations have confronted the differences of people who have very different physical appearance, language and cultural background, in which the problem has always been trying to keep the class and cultural differences from hardening over time into purely racial discrimination.

In Israel that is recognized as a danger because of the wide influction of Asian Jews, Oriental Jews, who, in appearance, are indistinguishable from, say, their East Indian counterparts or their Moroccan counterparts and the like and who represent about as far down on the cultural totem pole as you can get.

The big difference, of course, in Israel is that all of the resources in Israel are mobilized in the direction of overcoming this kind of development.

In Israel they develop structures, experimental and others to make sure—and they will tell you that they are fighting a race in which they may not win so that in time—that the Moroccan Jews, the Cochin Jews, the Hamite Jew, will not become the permanent dark skin lower order of permanent society. They work at it.

This is as near an illustration in modern times as I can find. What the committee is dealing with, the proposal, is part of that kind of effort.

As you yourself, noted earlier, and I think very aptly, we are interested in the whole history of the United States. It is not just history of the Negro which has been the sufferer here. It is the histories of the United States.

We speak of the Negro and his heroes. I submit that a white boy can find just as much in the history of Robert Small. He was a slave who with two or three slave companions stole a ship at the beginning of the Civil War from the Confederates and sailed to the Union side. He subsequently rose and he became a member of the South Carolina Legislature.

It is a magnificent story. Hollywood and television, looking for a good plot, couldn't find better ones than these instances.

Small was leading hundreds of slaves under the most undescribable hardships. This is the kind of stuff that makes a heroic narrative. Our whole Nation has been cheated of this kind of thing. Nobody knows about it.

I need not indicate, I am sure, that on a number of points Mr. Innis and I would find ourselves apart in the conception of our society and of the success or failure of the efforts that have been made today. We disagree about what the future holds, but his emphasis and Dr. Davis' emphasis on the necessity of having a positive and meaningful image for the Negro child to live up to is simply indisputable.

I have often said to audiences—and I return again to a Jewish theme here—that there is nothing more impressive in my opinion than the service of Passover, when the Jewish child from the time it is big enough to toddle to the chair and sit with the elders under circumstances of great solemnity is introduced, year in, year out, to the history of the exodus of his people from oppression of Egypt.

This story is told and retold and retold and by the time the Jewish child has reached his teens, it is part of him. There is no counterpart for this in the case of a Negro child.

There have been a great many efforts and they have been successful beyond what could have been reasonably anticipated from the resources available to them. The NAACP, for example, from the earliest days has made the learning and teaching of Negro history a cardinal part of its program.

The Association for the Study of Negro Life and History, which Carter Wilson founded 45 years ago, is another illustration. But these have been piecemeal.

We feel that we have had some success across the country in changing the climate in many public school systems toward the inclusion of textbooks and materials which are representative.

Our branch in Detroit had a 3-year battle with the Detroit Board of Education. They didn't get the history texts thrown out but they got a cracking good supplement developed which now is taught along with the history book. They don't refer to the history book because the corrections were so numerous.

We last summer published a book called "'Integrated School Books" which includes an annotated listing of some 399 school books which are illustrated in nature. We have already distributed I suppose some 15,000 copies to libraries and school departments across the country. It is a continuing part of our program.

Again, it has reached the stage where private voluntary efforts are simply inadequate to do the job that ought to be done. That is why we hail the bill and we hail the efforts of this committee.

We expect to give our fullest support to the bill hoping that it will be favorably reported out of the full committee and on to the floor of the House and that it will subsequently secure enactment. We will help vote for that bill. We believe in it.

Thank you very much.

Mr. SCHEUER. Thank you very much for your testimony, Mr. Morsell.

Mr. HATHAWAY. Thank you, Mr. Morsell.

I take it you disagree with Mr. Innis' statement that this would have to be an all-black commission.

Mr. MORSELL. I do disagree with that.

Mr. HATHAWAY. You think we should have experts in the field?

Mr. MORSELL. I think that it would be self-defeating if the commission were not fully representative of Negro expertise in this field. That is where the expertise largely is in the first place, not exclusively, but largely.

I fully agree, let me add, with the theory that this is a national responsibility and by that, of course, you may assume that I do not regard the future as a future in which hope lies only in a course of separateness.

I don't think, to be very candid with you, that anybody can sit anywhere today and guarantee that this Nation will be saved from disaster or that it will make its way through these troubled waters by any of the methods or approaches that have been discussed or are current or are being pushed nowadays by anybody.

I don't know who could guarantee it. I simply believe that the best hope, to the extent that there is hope, lies in an effort to approach a biracial society, a society without racial discrimination.

I happen to believe that you cannot do that by pursuing a racist course which seeks to build upon deplorable existing differences and try to make a virtue out of them alone and say, "We will go out separate ways because no matter how carefully or how eloquently you try to talk around it, this is the ultimate result of this." And so far as I know, nobody has developed a theory of governmental organization or society structure along the lines that Mr. Innis advocates which shows any signs of being more viable than what we are working for now.

I think that we differ in our estimates of the degree of success that we have had with some of our efforts today. I think if the history is better known—and this is another argument for this Commission—it will not appear to have been such a complete blank and such a complete failure.

It is what some of the critics today would have you believe.

Mr. SCHEUER. You say we have had some successes. Could you describe what the successes were briefly and what were the leverage points, what were the pressure points by which some institution changed its way of doing business.

Mr. MORSELL. Let us take the armed services, for example, as an immediate illustration of the latter point.

You don't hear very much about the integration of the Army and Air Force as an accomplishment or achievement, yet we know that in World War II, 20 years ago, we had two armies.

We had division-sized Negro units in World War II, the biggest we ever had. The other night I looked at a television broadcast showing the first two Negroes down in Orangeburg, S.C., going into the bowling alley that was the scene of the murder of the three students.

The interviewer spoke to two young white fellows who were there bowling with their group separately while the Negroes were bowling. Both of them, when they were asked, "How do you feel about this, do you want to continue to come here?" They both said, of course, they were going to continue to come and bowl.

One of them observed that one of the Negroes bowling looked pretty good. Both of them, however, said, "I was with them in the Army. I bowled with them in the Army. So what's the difference?"

Obviously, every white person with prejudices who went into the Army and served alongside Negroes for 6 months, a year, or 2 years, has not changed his attitude, has not become a flaming liberal on this question, but he has changed.

The extent to which he is ready to accept things that his father wouldn't accept is far greater. Let us agree that this is a slow, painfully slow, and maybe disastrously slow approach. It still cannot be said that there has not been change.

The state of the Negro in America in 1909 when the NAACP began would be incredible to the young Negro of today, because they were lynching us at the rate of one every 2 or 3 days—over a hundred a year.

In race riots all over the land they were killing Negroes by the score, burning their homes, driving them out of town. Ninety-five percent of Negroes in the South could not vote at all.

The few in the North had no leverage. If the Negro could not vote, he had no power at all. This route led to the breaking down of barriers to voting. Negroes by law in a large number of cities at that time were forced to live in only certain areas.

We had "ghettozation" by law and not de facto "ghettozation." You couldn't live somewhere else.

The Church of Richmond today, which Negroes bought in 1917 under times where you couldn't have Negroes where whites were, has one street that is a white street and the other a Negro street. The problem was that the door of the church was on the white block, and they had to close it and open up a door on the Negro side.

We knocked that kind of law out in 1918. We have gained in the area of criminal justice, in the area of voting, in the area of housing, the restrictive covenant—I suspect as a matter of fact that more Jews have benefited by this.

Mr. SCHEUER. How about in the area of the media which we are particularly concerned about, the radio, the television, the magazines, the press, the textbook publishing industry?

What have been the successes there and what were the leverages of power that made them change?

Mr. MORSELL. Let me say that I do not see mankind through rose-colored glasses; but by the same token I do not discount, and I think it is a serious error to discount, the existence of goodwill and decency in a great many people.

I think if you didn't have this, there isn't any prescription that would offer us the slightest hope. But structures and the like tend to inhibit its expression and to reduce it in size. With regard to media, the record has not been nearly as successful. In some other cases where you could bring the law to bear upon agencies of Government, you have always had much greater success.

We have been able to use with some success the Federal Communications Commission with regard to programing on television and radio. We have used, to perhaps even greater success, the threat or the implied threat of consumer reaction to products if something were not done to introduce a Negro figure here and there on a television ad. This has been spotty.

I am going to be testifying at the end of the week on this same matter. The progress has been very spotty. We have had a period of about 2 years ago, 3 years ago, when almost every time you tuned in your television set you would see a flash somewhere of a Negro in the background in a crowd or something and then all of a sudden that seems to have disappeared as though they had done their duty for 1966 and we will forget about it for 1967.

In the newspapers we have now reached a new controversy over the word "Negro" which I insist is a good word, probably the most accurate and exclusive of the words that are used. To get the capitalizing of the word Negro in general usage in the United States represented a complaint of I suppose 25 years.

That is an awful lot of time to have to take to accomplish that much of an achievement, and now that we are told it is going to be supplanted, and that there is this overwhelming opinion which I do not discern on the part of Negroes everywhere to have done with that and to call themselves black. It may turn out to have been a waste of time.

Mr. SCHEUER. I recall that E. B. White said that there is no such thing as black and white. It is all brown or pinky-grey.

Mr. MORSELL. As a purist in color I think that is true. This is an old controversy as you know. At the time of the founding of the NAACP the big question was to call it Afro-American or colored or Negro.

I don't understand why colored went out and we will have this argument over and over again I suspect as time passes.

Mr. SCHEUER. Dr. Morsell, you have given us a very interesting and very stimulating testimony. We thank you very much for your kindness in coming down.

We now would like to invite Mr. James Baldwin, the very distinguished playwright, to testify before us.

I should apologize that Mr. Baldwin was not on the schedule of witnesses; we had not expected he would be able to testify but are most pleased he can.

STATEMENT OF JAMES BALDWIN, ACCOMPANIED BY MRS. BETTY SHADAZZ

Mr. BALDWIN. I would like to make a suggestion before I begin. I brought with me Mrs. Betty Shadazz who is Malcolm X's widow.

Mr. SCHEUER. Would you like us to invite her to testify with you?

Mr. BALDWIN. Yes.

I am much in favor of the proposed legislation. I have to be honest with you and say that it occurs to me that the principal problem one faces in teaching Negroes their culture is that we will find that impossible to do without teaching American history, in the sense, then, for the first time. The burden under which the Negro child operates in this country, as your previous witnesses have indicated, is that he has no sense of identity.

It occurs to me that this involves a great national waste on the part of the morale of the child who is black. It appears to me that it is a great national waste not only for a Negro child but for any child growing up in this country. Anyone who is black is taught, as my generation was taught, that Negroes are not a civilization or culture, and that we came out of the jungle and were saved by the missionary.

Not only is this something awful to me, which eventually puts me on the street corner, but it's awful to everyone. You cannot educate a child if you first destroy his morale. That is why they leave school. You cannot educate him if he sees what is happening to his fathers, if he sees Ph. D.'s toting garbage.

If he sees in fact on the one hand no past and really no present and certainly no future, then you have created what the American public likes to think of, in the younger generation, as the nigger we invent and the nigger they invent. What has happened is that you destroy the child from the cradle.

Mr. SCHEUER. It is the institutionalization of the prophesy.

Mr. BALDWIN. If the cat cannot join a union no matter how many pennies he saves, he will still be at the bottom of the barrel. There is really nothing you can do with him. By and by, he will not listen to you and he will not listen to me. I am not a witness nor a hope. I am proof of what the country does to you if you are black. That is true even if I am Jackie Robinson.

Mr. SCHEUER. Do you think that this legislation in a minor way—none of us suggest that it is a great panacea—might bring together the talent that would produce a program to open up the doors of our education system, of our textbooks, of our media, to portray the role of the Negro in American life, and in world affairs so that the Negro would have an enhanced self-image and so that the white child would have a true sense of Negro contributions?

Mr. BALDWIN. That is the hope of the proposed bill. But we would be deluding ourselves if we did not understand that the particular history of my forefathers in this country can change the climate in this country. That climate is not one of flattery.

Mr. SCHEUER. I think the Anti-Riot Commission Report says that as it is, as you have been doing for many years.

Mr. BALDWIN. You have to face the fact that in the textbook industry—the key word there is "industry"—McGraw Hill is not yet about to destroy all its present textbooks and create new ones, because they will not be bought by the colleges and by the schools, at least not yet in St. Louis, or in Maryland, or New Orleans, or for that matter in New York. It is, after all, a profit-motive industry.

One cannot expect a business to put itself out of business under altruistic motives. One has got to find some way then, it would seem to me, to indicate to the textbook industry, which is a great stumbling block here, that would indicate to them that it is in their self-interest.

For example, the terrifying thing in the minds of the public was Malcolm X. One of the reasons you got Malcolm X was because when he was quite young and wanted to become a lawyer, his teacher advised him to do something that a colored person could do, like become a carpenter.

Only the child, or the brother or sister or the mother of that child knows what happens to that child's morale at that time. This is engrained in the American mythology. It will not be tomorrow that it is uprooted. We have to begin.

We are beginning late, I must say, but any beginning is better than none. But I don't think we should pretend that it is going to be easy.

Mr. SCHEUER. Can you give us any recommendations of yours as to how this proposal of ours can be improved and how it can be refined and how it can be given a clearer direction? Can you give us any insights as to how we can do the job better?

Mr. BALDWIN. If I were you and sitting where you are sitting, there are some people I would get in touch with. I would get in touch with Sterling Brown out of the University of Washington; I would talk to John Franklin. I am not in agreement with Mr. Innis entirely about this being an all-black commission. I would also talk to William Styron, but I would talk to people like Sterling Brown.

Mr. SCHEUER. Did you say you were not in agreement that it should be all Negro?

Mr. BALDWIN. I think it would be self-defeating. As I read it, it would be an attempt to teach American history. I am a little bit hard bitten about white liberals.

Mr. SCHEUER. Is that a pejorative phrase when you use it?

Mr. BALDWIN. It can be. I don't trust people who think of themselves as liberals. I do trust some white people, like Bill, he is not a Negro. He is a Deep Southern cat who had paid his dues and he has been through the fire and he knows what it is about. I trust him more than Max Lesher. What I am saying is that I don't trust missionaries.

I don't want anybody working with me because they are doing something for me. What I want them to do is to work in their own communities. I want you to tell your brothers and your sisters and your wife and your children what it is all about. Don't tell me because I know already. You see what I mean?

You have the power. But to answer you and go back to your question, I think one of the stumbling blocks is that the nature of the black experience in this country does indicate something about the total American history which frightens Americans. It brings up all those things you have talked about and want to talk about.

It brings up the real history of the country—the history of our relationships with Mexicans and slaves. All these points contradict the myth of American history. It attacks the American identity in a sense.

Shirley Temple would be a very different person if she were black.

Mr. SCHEUER. She probably would be a Member of Congress.

Mr. BALDWIN. We can't prove that by the Members of Congress. You see what I mean. Someone like Sterling Brown is an old poet and an old blues singer.

He knows more than, say, a man my age. He can tell you things which I cannot, about you and me. It is a level of experience about which Ray Charles sings and of which all Americans are still terrified.

If we are going to build a multiracial society, which is our only hope, then one has got to accept that I have learned a lot from you and a lot of it is bitter, but you have a lot to learn from me and a lot of that will be bitter. That bitterness is our only hope. That is the only way we get past it. Am I making sense to you?

Mr. SCHEUER. Absolutely.

Congressman Gus Hawkins of California.

Mr. HAWKINS. I must apologize for being called out of the room, Mr. Baldwin.

I certainly think that you have offered some very wonderful suggestions and some good comments. I particularly enjoyed what I considered to be the point that you made that the objective of such a commission would be to teach American history, making it plain and clear that the history of the black man in America is that part of American history. There is not reason to separate it.

You feel that competent persons, both black and white, should be engaged in doing this?

Mr. BALDWIN. It is our common history. My history is also yours.

Mr. HAWKINS. I certainly agree with you, Mr. Baldwin. I certainly appreciate this opportunity that you have afforded us.

Mr. SCHEUER. Congressman Hathaway of Maine.

Mr. HATHAWAY. Mr. Baldwin, I would take it that you would agree that perhaps we should expand the scope of the bill to cover not only the history of the culture but also the contemporary heroes.

Mr. BALDWIN. Yes, but you must understand that, speaking as black Americans, my heroes have always been from the point of view of white Americans as bad niggers. Cassius Clay is one of my heroes but not one of yours.

I on the other hand am not suggesting that this Commission should establish a half of fame for great Negroes at all. What I am trying to suggest is that you recognize the role that my heroes—as distinguished from yours—have played in American life and the reasons why all my heroes came to such bloody ends.

From my point of view, Mohammad Ali Clay, without discussing his affiliations or what I may think of him has been hanged by the public as a bad nigger. He is going to be an example to every other Negro man. Those are my heroes. Those are not the heroes of the American public. You will find yourself up against that fact before many days have passed.

Do you see what I mean? As long as my heroes are not yours, then the bitterness in the ghetto increases hour by hour and grows more and more dangerous and does not only blow up the ghetto but blows up the cities.

When I came back from New York a few weeks ago, I came back during the garbage strike when all New York looked just like Harlem.

Mr. SCHEUER. It looked just like south Bronx, the district I represent, and I was happy to see the rest of the city have what the residents of Harlem and Bedford-Stuyvesant put up with 365 days of the year. It was a salutory experience.

Mr. BALDWIN. When you unleash a plague it covers the entire city and Nation. What has been happening to me all of these years is now beginning to happen to all of you, and this was inevitable. What we are involved with here is an attempt to have ourselves, and we need each other for that.

My history, though, contains the truth about America. It is going to be hard to teach it.

Mr. HATHAWAY. Perhaps we should tell more of the truth about our heroes, such as George Washington and Abraham Lincoln, who are built up in history books almost as myths. We know that they had frailties. We know that they made a lot of mistakes. Those mistakes are never built up, so that the white man has the impression immediately that his heroes are almost gods.

Mr. BALDWIN. I don't think that any kid believes any of those legends about George Washington and his cherry tree—I cannot tell a lie, and all that nonsense.

Mr. HATHAWAY. I think at certain stages they do. After a while they get to believe that it is not true.

Mr. BALDWIN. I never did.

This is fine. I think it does a disservice to a child to tell him things which are not true. Children cannot really be fooled. For example, and I will be very brief, you remember that several years ago the Birmingham church school was bombed and there were four girls killed in there. They were not killed by some madman, but by a mad society which is not only located in Birmingham. At that time some of us threw together an ad hoc committee to prevent celebrations on Christmas Day.

We had lost the right as a Christian nation to celebrate the birth of Christ. I discovered during this that Santa Claus is not needed by children, but by grownups. People say we couldn't do that because the children would be so upset. The fact is that it wasn't true; what they really meant was that they would be upset.

We give them those legends and they try to survive them, but no kid has ever believed anything written about George Washington. Anyway, even if they did, by the time they are 17 they have got to revise their whole estimate of reality around the fact of human beings, not legends.

I think the sooner one learns the truth, the better. Do I make myself clear?

Mr. HATHAWAY. I am just wondering whether I agree with you. Perhaps we just need a more realistic appraisal of what our heroes should be.

Mr. BALDWIN. Anyway, leaving aside the hypothetical matters, the black kid in the ghetto doesn't believe in these heroes for a moment. You begin the process of the breakdown of communication virtually from the cradle.

I really didn't believe at the time I was seven the Pledge of Allegiance, and no black boy I knew did, either. For very good reasons, too. I didn't believe it, in effect, because the country didn't believe it. I didn't believe it because you didn't believe it.

If you had believed it, I would have been in a different place. My father would have been a very different man. You didn't believe it, so I didn't. You can't fool a kid. You still don't believe it, and so they don't, and they won't believe it until you do. You have to prove that you do.

Mr. HATHAWAY. By action?

Mr. BALDWIN. Yes. Let me get a job, allow me the right to protect my women, my house, my children. That is all the Negro wants: his autonomy. Nobody hates you. The time is far gone for that. I simply want to live my life.

I suggest, too, that the kids all up and down this country in the streets of all our cities are coming to ruin and are going on the needle. They are coming to nothing. This is a waste no country can afford.

I am the flesh of your flesh and bone of your bone; I have been here as long as you have been here—longer—I paid for it as much as you have. It is my country, too. Do recognize that that is the whole question. My history and culture has got to be taught. It is yours.

Mr. HATHAWAY. Do you think that there is some hope that if the culture is brought back to white America that the black America has a better chance?

Mr. BALDWIN. Yes, This would involve a change in your institutions. It is not just a matter of passing a bill. The Christian Church in this country is a very popular institution. But this has always been a racist institution, and we take this as immoral.

Once I become a part of that church, that institution is a different institution. It is not a matter of letting me into it, it has to change. This is true for all American institutions—including schools and the textbook industry.

You are to accept the fact that I am the darker brother, and the key word there is brother. Whereas you from Europe came here voluntarily, I was kidnapped, and my history was destroyed here. For your purposes, this has to be faced. I am not trying to be bitter or anything. This is the way it is.

Mr. SCHEUER. I would like to emphasize that we are in entire accord with you in that we want the institutions to change. We want the textbook industry to change; we want the teaching industry to change. We want the radio and television and press industry to change, and we hope that this Commission could start to do the hard intellectual work and play the leadership role to induce change.

This Commission, if it is anything, will be a change effort. We would like to have your views on how it can best be achieved to perfect the design of this Commission so that it will open up doors.

Mr. BALDWIN. I am not gifted in this area. Let me offer a suggestion. You can do whatever you like with it. We are talking about mass media. One is up against this: There is a very successful movie going around which I saw a few days ago in Hollywood. It is called, "Guess Who's Coming To Dinner."

This movie is about an interracial marriage, I suppose. Sidney Poitier plays a very beautiful and modest role. That is all he ever plays. This is the mass media for you.

Now if one is going to deal with the mass media, you have to be aware that you are reaching two publics: the white people in this country and abroad; I talked to some people in London who adored it and think it is true. But, of course, when I watch it, some cat in the ghetto is watching; it may do great things for your morale, but it does terrible things to him.

He recognizes that the movie is a copout. Mr. Poitier is not an ordinary citizen. It obviously would be a different movie if he were able to play a real man.

I am not overstating my case; the movie does say that in order for me to marry this particular white chick, I have to be what he is in the movie. Well, that is not so of any white person, he can marry whomever he wants to marry. I am trying to say that the structure of the mass media is such that I think you ought to be aware that there would be a tremendous resistance.

You will hear what I have heard for years. It is great and powerful but it is not for our readers. Or—it is a risky picture and we can't do it. The mass media is mainly a form of escape, and someone said many, many years ago that no white person is going to make his escape personality black, especially in this country. I don't think we should be deluded about that.

Mr. SCHEUER. Here exactly is that kind of a challenge that we hope the Commission will face squarely.

Mr. BALDWIN. We are terribly penalized in this country, every single one of us, famous and obscure. It is like being what America still considers one of your niggers. This Commission has to begin to break down that terrifying heritage, which, after all, destroys the white child, too.

Mr. SCHEUER. That was the point I was trying to make with Mr. Innis before you came. The 90-percent white majority has as much or more of an interest in this purification process, because they are deprived by not knowing of Negro history and culture.

Mr. BALDWIN. They are frightened. I don't hate white people; I don't have to. I am not afraid of you. You face a Southern deputy, and he does hate you—because he is scared to death of you. He is the one who is in trouble, and that is the man you have to liberate.

Mr. SCHEUER. We can't thank you enough for coming to see us. You certainly deserve the door prize for having come the longest distance. We are grateful, and we benefited enormously by your views.

Mrs. SHADAZZ. I am in complete accord with this bill and in teaching black history in the schools. Some of the things I have heard I have disagreed with, and some I have agreed with. I think primarily the problem is one of getting black history in the schools. If it is wanted by blacks and whites, I think this would solve some of the problems, if cooperation is wanted.

This is needed to curb the things that are going on and some terrible things that will continue to go on. I think a lot of the hysteria has been created primarily by whites who basically have not understood blacks, who have not treated them as human beings.

Everyone has basic emotions of hate, fear, and love, and I think the whites in this country have used the machinery of propaganda very skillfully. You find blacks who want to know something about their history and you find whites who don't understand or who are fearful. They will publicize this sort of thing as a hate gathering and a hate meeting, when actually it could possibly be a historical meeting that whites and blacks could learn from.

94-721 O—68——4

I think if black history was taught properly, that a lot of whites who throw around their superiority so lavishly wouldn't do so. Blacks didn't come to this country voluntarily, and I think they have worked a long time for no pay. The least that could be done is that the proper history be taught.

I don't think it is right to alienate Mr. Innis. I think he wants black history taught as well as anyone else, black or white. It is a necessity at this time. However, I feel, like Mr. Baldwin, that black history should be taught in schools from slavery to now.

However, I do feel that institutions could be set up that taught black history that goes back say, to the neolithic and paleolithic period. I feel that there might possibly be two institutions. I think that American history should be taught for all, but separate institutions could be set up for history other than this.

I was very surprised when a white female woman I admired told me recently that she just found out that 3 years ago the blacks in this country actually came from Africa. She has degrees by the basketful, and I wondered what school she went to.

Mr. SCHEUER. I wonder where she thought they came from.

Mrs. SHADAZZ. This is not to criticize her, because she is a very educated woman and one of the pillars of your American society. I feel that whites should learn about blacks as much as blacks are forced to learn about whites.

Mr. SCHEUER. I am very glad you made that point because it is a point that we feel very deeply about. The purposes and the goals of our Commission are, namely, to propagate the contributions that blacks have made to world history and to our own history and culture. This is just as important for our white society as it is for the Negro members of our society. All of us are deprived and all of us are impoverished, perhaps unequally. Certainly all of us suffer the detrimental effects of the lack of consciousness in our society, in our education system, in our media, of the contributions that Negroes have made and are making today.

I am very happy to have you make that point. I want to thank you very much for your kindness and generosity in giving us your views.

Mr. BALDWIN. I don't at all want to isolate Roy Innis. I disagree with him as a tactical disagreement.

Mr. SCHEUER. We agreed a great deal on what he said.

It is now 1 o'clock. We have run behind schedule, mostly due to the fact that we have had such stimulating and provocative witnesses. We will adjourn until 2:15 and then we will start again with John Harmon and Dr. John Davis and go through the rest of the witness list.

(Whereupon, at 1 p.m., the committee recessed, to reconvene at 2:15 p.m., the same day.)

AFTER RECESS

Mr. SCHEUER. The Select Subcommittee on Labor is hereby convened.

Our first witness will be John Harmon. He is the president of the Westchester chapter of the Association for the Study of Negro Life and History.

We are very happy to have you with us, Mr. Harmon.

Do you have a prepared statement?

Mr. HARMON. I don't have a prepared statement because I didn't get notification of this. I have some notes and will submit a statement to the committee.

Mr. SCHEUER. Your entire statement will be printed at this point in the record.

Mr. HARMON. I will be speaking from notes.

Mr. SCHEUER. We have eight witnesses for the afternoon session, so we are going to ask all of the witnesses to summarize their thoughts and speak as briefly as they can.

Mr. Harmon, we are delighted to have you. You can proceed.

STATEMENT OF JOHN HARMON, PRESIDENT OF WESTCHESTER CHAPTER, ASSOCIATION FOR THE STUDY OF NEGRO LIFE AND HISTORY

Mr. HARMON. Mr. Chairman and members of the committee, I am president of the Westchester County chapter, which is affiliated with the national organization in Washington. We cover the entire Westchester County. Since our chapter was organized in 1965, we have been busily engaged in the same purposes as this bill proposes, disseminating information with regard to the history and culture of African Americans, carrying on an active program on the question of textbooks in the schools, and trying to integrate Negro culture in the schools of Westchester.

I think significantly enough, that as a result of a resolution that was adopted by our chapter in June of last year, which was sent to the Constitutional Convention of the State of New York, a hearing was called.

As a result of our activities and—before going into that—it has been out theory that it is the people who will get things moving. Within our chapter we have attempted to involve the entire community in the whole question of people's culture. It doesn't belong to the elite, it belongs to everyone.

Mr. SCHEUER. Did we supply you with a copy of this bill?

Mr. HARMON. Yes.

Mr. SCHEUER. Do you have any specific view or counsel that you can give us on the bill itself as to how we can improve it, whether you favor it, whether there are any parts of it that you are skeptical about, how we can fortify it?

Mr. HARMON. I do want to call your attention to the specific activities that have been carried on by us.

I have a letter from the Greenburg District School No. 8. I was at the superintendent's office this morning before coming here.

Mr. SCHEUER. Mr. Harmon, this committee is having a hearing on a particular bill that has a particular purpose, and what we would like you to do is give us your views on whether you think the bill is workable. Give us any ideas that you may have on how we can improve the bill and how we can achieve a machinery for collecting and disseminating the contributions of Negroes to our lives and history.

If you could direct your thoughts to this bill and give us your counsel and advice as to how we can make it better, giving us your critical reaction to parts of it perhaps that are not as sound as they might be, that would be particularly helpful to us.

Mr. HARMON. That is precisely what I was getting to. The reason that I mentioned this is that in the Westchester County area, in cooperation with the Greenburg School District, an Afro-American culture and art center is being established as of December of this year under title II. This is in cooperation with the New York State Education Department and I just thought maybe you might like to hear about this—the dissemination of information and the methods by which it might be done.

I think that this would be specifically a recommendation. The purpose of this project which we have undertaken is an accurate, independent collection of Negro history and culture.

Implement parochial and private schools' needs in this area with relevant curriculum services. Make available to all residents of the county the history and culture of 10 percent of its national population. Provide information and education for both the white and Negro.

I want to say on this point that we have been able to get the State of New York to issue what is known as curriculum K–212, and K–212 is an integration of the cultural contributions of all the people in the State's population from kindergarten to the 12th grade.

We have contended that it should not be separated, but should be made a part of the history and the culture of the people.

So, that one of the things that I had thought of in discussing it, and I discussed this bill with about 20 leaders throughout Westchester County and with Congressman Ottinger, a member of your committee, and I am well acquainted with him.

Mr. SCHEUER. An outstanding Member of Congress.

Mr. HARMON. He is with us on these matters. The reason why I mention this is because this is the only county in the State where a county itself has sponsored a museum of Negro art and culture, which will open in 1969 as a result of an appropriation through title II and through the State education part.

We feel that one way to get this information across is to involve the total community, parents' associations, the lodges, the schools, and all the people. In testifying before the State constitutional convention we tried to point out one thing. That is, that it is all right to keep it on a scholarly level and keep it in the classroom, but when we get out in the street and have to deal with a policeman or have to go to the bank and borrow money, the first thing a man looks at is not your ability, but he looks at your color and decides that this is a factor.

My grandfather owned about 40 acres of land in the city of Houston and this land was valueless as long as my grandfather owned it, but as soon as somebody else owned it it jumped up 1,000 percent in value. These are some of the problems that we have had to contend with over the years in the struggles that come out of the very little people.

We talk about the ghettos. Ghettos and the underprivileged and the minorities. It would be a very simple thing to do away with this, with the proper understanding that would come through the contributions of people.

I am particularly interested in the economic aspects of this because when you look back at the whole spectrum of American history and take into consideration the contributions of the Negro people as slaves to the economy of America and then try to translate this into terms of dollars and cents, the value of this would be tremendous.

I wrote my thesis at Columbia on the question of farm credit in the United States and we tried to go into this question of the value of the labor that was expended free of charge in this slave period. Also, there was a question of the connection of Africa with America in the textbooks, and we worked with this considerably, and this is an area which I feel that the Commission ought to go into.

In the textbooks, where there is no connection between Africa and America, there is a terrific gap which affects white children as well as Negro children, and Negro children feel as if there is no past.

I know one teacher at White Plains High School asked, "Where do the textbooks start in America?" Let us start with slavery, and this is not necessarily true. There was Estavenico, who was with Columbus and so forth and so on.

Therefore, it is extremely important in attacking the textbook question that this area be covered more thoroughly. In regard to what could this Commission do, first of all, I think it should not be temporary as it is proposed. I think it should be a permanent commission and it should be legislated to make it permanent, with power to act just as the Federal Trade Commission, and so forth and so on.

Here is the danger in making it a temporary commission to issue another study and report. It will be perhaps carried to Congress, but it will be maybe 3 or 4 or 5 years before real action is taking place. It would appear to me and to those I have discussed it with, it would be far better if we could implement this by making it something permanent with the power to act and to go into the local communities.

Mr. SCHEUER. Our purpose in establishing this Commission is not to decide what the final program should be. That is what the Commission is going to do. The Commission may decide that there ought to be a permanent agency in business that would work on this over a considerable period of time, and if they make that recommendation, then it will be up to the Congress to act on it.

We don't want to prejudge for the Commission what should be the ultimate program.

Do you basically support the concept of the Commission?

Mr. HARMON. Oh, yes. That is why we brought for the Commission a copy of the report of the Westchester Art Center so that they could see for themselves what is already being accomplished, and that is why I kept talking about it, and the Greenburg School District sent a letter to the committee in support of this.

Naturally, you couldn't expect us not to want to support such an effort. I am only telling you how we as people feel it should be implemented. We feel, in addition to this, that wider publicity should be given to what this select subcommittee is doing, so that more people will testify—more people from the streets and more people from the little peoples' organizations, parents' organizations, who are dealing with this and dealing with guidance counselors in school. They give our children an awful lot of trouble.

Mr. SCHEUER. Congressman Hathaway.

Mr. HATHAWAY. How long has your study been going on?

Mr. HARMON. For 2½ years. This particular commission that has been set up in Westchester County. There was a meeting held in December, the eighth, and already the grant has been approved in Albany for the establishment of a Westchester Museum of Art and Culture.

There will be books, selections of all kinds. I think the first appropriation was a $50,000 appropriation to get it started.

I think this is something very practical and the very kind of the thing you are talking about. It is a thing that counties and cities and other districts could recommend to have in its establishment. It is something like the Human Rights Commission that has local committees and districts and whatnot.

I think that this would be extremely important, also—an involvement. I heard Mr. Baldwin talking about the question of whether it should be Negro and white. I think our experience is a good one in Westchester, where you are supposed to have all these wealthy people and elites and so forth. We have been able to involve the school districts. We have been able to involve people in Hartsdale, Scarsdale, and so forth in our activities.

In Scarsdale Junior High School we have a member who is actively teaching a group of white students on a volunteer basis about Negro history, and his name is Irving Sloane, and he is quite an authority on this field.

Mr. HAWKINS. I have no questions.

Mr. SCHEUER. Mr. Harmon, we very much appreciate your coming down here and your views have been most interesting, and you can be sure that we will take them very much into account. Thank you again for coming here.

I would now like to call Mr. Malvin Goode of the ABC Television Network.

STATEMENT OF MALVIN GOODE, ABC-TV, NEW YORK

Mr. GOODE. Mr. Chairman, I would like to thank you for giving me preference over my distinguished friend and colleagues. I have a short statement about 8 or 9 minutes long that I would like to read. When I finish, I will be happy to submit myself for questioning.

Mr. SCHEUER. Your statement will be put in the record at this point.

STATEMENT OF MALVIN GOODE, ABC-TV, NEW YORK

Gentlemen, my name is Malvin Goode, I live at 80 Howland Avenue in Teaneck, New Jersey and I am employed by the American Broadcasting Company as one of its correspondents at the United Nations. During the past six years I have been given other assignments which have carried me to forty one states and nine foreign countries and it has been my privilege to interview Prime Ministers, Foreign Ministers, our President and more than fifty of your own colleagues in the House and Senate regarding various issues and problems affecting our country and the world at large.

I am the father of six children, the eldest a graduate of Penn State and presently a Captain in the Air Force and stationed in Honolulu where he was assigned after spending a year in Southeast Asia as a Radar specialist and for his work there was awarded the bronze star. The second son is a Program Coordinator for the Mellon Bank and Trust Company in Pittsburgh but currently is on loan to our

Federal government in its Plans-For-Progress program. The third son is a graduate of West Virginia University and presently is employed by the state of Pennsylvania. My next oldest is a junior at Virginia Union University, her younger brother is a junior at Huston-Tillotson College in Austin, Texas and the baby, 15 years of age, is a sophomore in Teaneck High School.

I was born in Virginia but spent all of my childhood, adolescence and most of my adult life in the steel-producing area of Pittsburgh, Pennsylvania, and attended elementary & secondary schools there as well as the University of Pittsburgh where I completed work for a Bachelor's Degree in 1931. I was employed in the Homestead works of U.S. Steel for 12 years while in high school and college and five years after college and never received one single promotion in that period of time.

I hope you will forgive time given to this background but it should serve as a basis for my willingness to testify before this committee with my hope that I can contribute something to furthering passage of this most important legislation the House Bill No. 12962 which calls for the establishment of a Commission on Negro History and Culture whose function shall be to create a better understanding and knowledge of Negro history and culture. I would underscore two of the proposed commission's tasks—"unearthing, preserving and collecting historical materials dealing with Negro history and culture" and "methods of disseminating such materials so that the information can be best integrated into the mainstream of American education and life" and may I add American history.

At this point I want to immodestly point out to the committee that it has been my privilege to work with Negro youth either as a layman, or as a professional for almost forty years. This interest began with teaching Sunday School in the twenties, then two years as a Juvenile Court Probation Officer, five years as Director of Boys Work at the Pittsburgh YMCA, six years as Manager of a Public Housing Development with a strong Youth Program and eighteen years in Radio and the Journalistic profession. In the past five years since coming to New York I have been to classrooms and Assemblies at more than fifty secondary schools and colleges to talk with our Youth and I know what it means to feel a sense of pride in being an American, but more important I know particularly what it means, with pride, to be an Afro-American. This pride, however, did not come from what I learned in textbooks or instructors in secondary school or at the University. It developed late in life from travel and extensive reading of the history of Black America and most of the material came from the pens of Afro-Americans—Carter G. Woodson, E. Franklin Frazier, Charles Wesley and others. The textbooks I used in those days carried usually one line about Booker T. Washington and occasionally an item about a great American scientist, Dr. George Washington Carver, and once in a great while some reference was made to Frederick Douglass. The encyclopaediae we used for reference in our high school and college work did not mention a SoJourner Truth, nor Toussaint L'Overture, Paul Laurence Dunbar, Countee Cullen, Crispus Attucks or Dr. Daniel Hale Williams. I was forty years of age before I knew Benjamin Banneker drew the plans for the city of Washington, D.C. or that Garrett Morgan invented the traffic light in Cleveland in 1923, or that Jan Matzlinger invented the electrically operated shoe repair machinery.

In the history of this nation's conflicts since 1776 only recently published history books have noted there were black soldiers with General Andrew Jackson and black sailors with Commodore Perry in the War of 1812; I have yet to read in an encyclopedia or history book that President Lincoln said in 1862—"The use of colored troops constitutes the heaviest blow yet dealt to the rebellion and that at least one of these important successes could not have been achieved but for the aid of Black Soldiers." Most histories do not record that at the battle of Chapin's Farm, September 29, 1864, thirteen Black soldiers won the Congressional Medal of Honor nor that a Black regiment, the 62nd U.S. Infantry fired the last shot in the Civil War at Brownsville, Texas May 13, 1865. It is not generally known that Theodore Roosevelt fought the battle of San Juan Hill with Black Soldiers; General Pershing used black soldiers to put down the Mexican Insurrection in Carnizales, Mexico in 1916, and the history of World War I and the battles of Chateau Thierry and the Argonne Forest might not have been won without black soldiers in segregated units. Surely I need not remind you of 1941 to 1945 and the record shows 1,400 Black boys are buried at the Battle of the Bulge alone and it is most unfortunate that few historians are recording the events in Korea just fifteen years ago when out of the 53,000 casualties, 7,800 of them were black boys.

If this commission is established and does its work well the history books of the future will surely carry the information that as of March 18, 1968 in Viet Nam **almost 90,000 of the 510,000** American boys in those rice paddies were black boys.

To give you another example of the wilful and what seems to have been the planned negligence and oversight, we speak proudly and freely of the Dr. Jonas Salk vaccine and projects and buildings have been named for him because of his work to control polio, but none hears of the Dr. Charles Drew Blood Plasma and can we begin to count the millions whose lives have been saved by the work of this medical genius . . . a brown skin physician who worked tirelessly at Howard University to produce and perfect the theory of Blood Plasma which has led to the establishment of Blood Banks all over the world. Today we pay homage to some doctors for the heart transplant which has not yet been too successful, but more than fifty years ago with limited facilities, Dr. Daniel Hale Williams performed the first successful operation on the heart and his patient lived many years thereafter. Have you heard of a Daniel Hale Clinic or Hospital?

The program your bill proposes will do much to eliminate this deliberate void in our nation's history and even more important, this knowledge should serve to help narrow-minded and bigoted Americans to understand that black people have played a most important part in the development of this nation in every area of its life. It naturally will give a black child a new sense of pride by setting the record straight—a record that for generations has been blotted out of the pages of our history and textbooks in the classrooms and libraries.

I will not burden this committee with personal instances of what it is like to be considered "less than" an American by people who did not know and many still do not know what black people have meant to this nation. This lack of knowledge of history, coupled with an almost inherent, unsupported feeling of superiority has made life so tragic for many of us . . . denial of jobs, denial of promotions, refused service in public accommodations, downgrading by a teacher or professor in high school and college, abuse by authorities, illegal jailings . . . hundreds of instances designed to make one feel inferior and to keep one inferior. I am positive Congressmen Nix, Diggs and Hawkins . . . your colleagues, like myself, bear psychological scars until today because of this kind of inferior treatment by those who believed themselves superior because they did not know that a Dr. Charles Drew discovery just might have saved the life of a loved one, or that they stop now at a traffic light because of a black man, Garrett Morgan. I don't want this committee to feel that I live in the past. Such is not the case, but the present is only in a limited way, improved over the past, and America will never gain her full potential until 15% of her population has the same treatment, the same opportunity, the same "open doors" that are accorded other Americans, most of them whose roots go back to other countries. The history of Africans and Americans of African descent has been distorted, belittled, ignored and submerged in the education of Black and White children in this country. Because of it, this very day, we are tortured with a threatened revolution that emanates from the struggle of black Americans for human rights and dignity. That revolution has already caused the deaths of almost one hundred persons and property damage which approaches a billion dollars, and the end is not in sight unless we move rapidly toward the establishment of Equality with a capital "E". Such a bill as you gentlemen propose could be an important part of movements currently in progress all over the country to offset any further holocausts.

My friend Whitney Young has put it so well he said . . . "If you would not have angry men in the streets you must make those streets avenues of hope and not despair." Tolstoi said several centuries ago "You don't hurt a man when you deny him, you hurt him when you make him no longer care." I can think of no better way to make a young black boy or girl, man or woman really care than to let them understand you count them as important cogs in the wheel of American life and what better way than to make him cognizant and be cognizant yourself of the part his forbearers have played in bringing this country to its present position of economic and social growth. If you would dare wage a non-violent war against the worst evil which afflicts and threatens to destroy us, I urge you to pass this legislation as one of the key weapons to unite America. So many are prone to speak glibly and loosely about "Freedom, Justice and Equality", but in their hearts there is no fullness of meaning for they lack respect for their Black brothers. This lack is due primarily to their limited knowledge of what Black people have contributed.

In the words of Sidney Willhel and Edwain Powell. The Negro is not challenging basic American values. He wants to join the system, not upset it; he wants to come into the house, not bomb it, and he feels an inherent right to come into that house because he helped to build it. One of the problems is that White America who moved into that house has no knowledge of Black America who helped to build it. Martin Luther King wrote from his Birmingham jail that Negroes "are forever fighting a degenerating sense of "nobodiness". The issue, gentlemen, is one of human, as well as civil rights, and it involves mutual respect for each other. This respect is only possible when each values the comradship, the cooperation, the help of the other. If the help, the cooperation, the work of the Black man is submerged, is hidden, is ignored, then we can never bring the light of reason and the good sense of humanity to bear upon the blindness and ignorance and prejudices which beget the hatred that afflicts our society today. The United Nations General Assembly passed the Universal Declaration of Human Rights in 1948, twenty years ago which has as its purpose . . . "to promote and encourage respect for human rights and fundamental freedoms for all without distinction of race, sex, language, or religion." This declaration was designed for the world but I'm certain it would apply to our nation as well. Let us join with others at work to ease the torture which afflicts us by establishing this instrument that will do so much to promote and encourage mutual respect for human rights and fundamental freedoms for all without distinction of race, sex, language or religion."

Thank you.

Mr. GOODE. I just wanted to give a little background so that they might understand why I was pleased to come before the Committee. I would like to see some kind of legislation passed that would establish or at least undergird committees that have been established to create some better understanding in this country of Negro history and culture.

I would like to underscore two of the proposed tasks as outlined in the bill. One is unearthing, preserving, and collecting historical materials dealing with Negro history and culture and, two, methods of disseminating such materials; so that the information can be best integrated into the mainstream of American education and life, and I may add, American history.

I have had a great deal of experience in working with youngsters over the past 40 years and in the past 5 years since coming to New York, I have been to classrooms and assemblies in more than 50 secondary schools and colleges to talk with particular Negro youth. I know personally what it means to feel a sense of pride in being an Afro-American. Of course, I want to point out to this committee that this pride did not come from what I learned in textbooks 40 years ago, either at high school or at the university. Most of the material came from the pens of Afro-Americans, men like Carter G. Woodson, E. Franklin Frazier, and Dr. Charles Wesley, who is in the audience today.

The textbooks I used in those days carried usually one line about Booker T. Washington and occasionally an item about a great American scientist, Dr. George Washington Carver, and once in a great while some reference was made to Frederick Douglass, and late in the 40's they began to mention a man by the name of Ralph Bunche. After them came Jackie Robinson and Willie Mays.

The encyclopedia we used for reference in our high school and college work did not mention a SoJourner Truth, nor Toussaint L'Overture, Paul Laurence Dunbar, Countee Cullen, Crispus Attucks or Dr. Daniel Hale Williams. I was 40 years of age before I knew Benjamin

Banneker drew the plans for the city of Washington, D.C., or that Garrett Morgan invented the traffic light in Cleveland in 1923, or that Jan Matzlinger invented the electric-operated shoe repair machine.

In the history of this Nation's conflicts since 1776, only recently published history books have noted that there were black soldiers with Gen. Andrew Jackson and black sailors with Commodore Perry in the War of 1812. Even in 1862, President Lincoln made this statement, "The use of colored troops constitutes the heaviest blow yet dealt to the rebellion and that at least one of these important successes could not have been achieved but for the aid of Black Soldiers."

Most histories that I have read do not record that at the Battle of Chapin's Farm, September 29, 1864, 13 black soldiers won the Congressional Medal of Honor, nor that a black regiment, the 62d U.S. Infantry, fired the last shot in the Civil War at Brownsville, Tex., May 13, 1865.

It is not generally known that Teddy Roosevelt fought the Battle of San Juan Hill, principally with black soldiers. At the Argonne Forest, and I need not remind the older ones in this audience that from 1941 to 1945 black soldiers were there, the record shows 1,400 boys are buried at the Battle of the Bulge alone.

It is most unfortunate that few historians are recording the events in Korea, just 15 years ago, when out of the 53,000 casualties, 7,800 of them were black boys. I hope that the history books that will be written in the future will point out that as of March 18, 1968, that of the 510,000 American boys in the rice paddies in Vietnam, 90,000 of them were black boys.

Mr. SCHEUER. I think 20 percent of the fatalities.

Mr. GOODE. We speak as Americans so proudly and freely of the Dr. Jonas Salk vaccine, and projects and buildings have been named for him because of his work to control polio.

But I haven't yet heard of Charles Drew High School. It is somewhere in the South. We can't begin to count the millions of lives that have been saved by the work of this medical genious, a brown skin physician who worked tirelessly at Harvard to produce and perfect the theory of blood plasma.

Today we pay homage to some doctors for the heart transplant, which has not yet been too successful. But more than 50 years ago, with limited facilities, Dr. Daniel Hale Williams performed the first successful operation on the heart, and his patient lived many years thereafter. Have we ever heard of a Daniel Hale Clinic or Hospital?

The proposed bill will do much to eliminate this deliberate void in our Nation's history. Even more important, this should serve to help narrow-minded and bigoted Americans to understand that black people have played a most important part in the development of this Nation in every area of its life.

Of course, it naturally will give a black child a new sense of pride by setting the record straight. I will not burden this Committee with personal instances of what it is like to be considered less than an American by people who did not know and many still do not know what black people have meant to this Nation.

I have had many experiences of working with people. I have had them in the last 6 years since I have been with ABC. I have gone into places to speak where people have said, "Are you looking for somebody?" I would say, "No, not particularly."

Then I would say, "I would like to see the Chairman." Before it is over with, there is all kinds of apologies, but before they knew I was with ABC–TV, I was just another black person who wandered into the room.

I am amazed sometimes at foreigners, those who come here on a 1- and 2-year visa, who shortly after they have been here 1, 2, or 3 months, adopt the idea of most white Americans that we are something less and you only become special when you have a sign on your back that you are Jackie Robinson, Mal Goode, or you are Bob Teague in CBS.

It is this kind of thing. This has come about because of a system that has been in existence for many, many generations where we have been denied proper positions, denied jobs, refused service and public accommodations, downgraded by our professor or teacher in high school or college, abused by authorities, suffered illegal jailings—hundreds of instances designed to make one feel inferior and to keep one inferior.

I don't want this Committee to feel that I live in the past. I want to make that clear. Such is not the case. But the present is only in a limited way improved over the past. I say very frankly that America will never gain her full potential, until 15 percent of her population has the same treatment, the same opportunity, the same "open doors" that are accorded other Americans—whose roots go back to other countries. The history of Africans and Americans of African descent has been distorted, belittled, ignored, and submerged in the education of black and white children in this country.

Because of it, this very day, we are tortured with a threatened revolution that emanates from the struggle of black Americans for human rights and dignity. That revolution has already caused the deaths of almost 100 persons and property damage which approaches a billion dollars, and the end is not in sight unless we move rapidly toward the establishment of equality with a capital "E."

Such a bill as proposed here could be an important part of movements that are currently in progress all over the country to offset any further holocausts. These movements unfortunately have come late.

My friend Whitney Young has put it so well when he said, "If you would not have angry men in the streets, you must make those streets avenues of hope and not despair." Tolstoi said several centuries ago, "You don't hurt a man when you deny him, you hurt him when you make him no longer care." I can think of no better way to make a young black boy or girl, man or woman, really care than to let them understand you count them as important cogs in the wheel of American life. And what better way, than to make him cognizant and be cognizant yourself of the part of his forbearers have played in bringing this country to its present position of economic and social growth. If you would dare wage a nonviolent war against the worst evil which afflicts and threatens to destroy us, I urge you to pass this legislation as one of the key weapons to unite America.

So many of us are prone to speak glibly and loosely about freedom and justice and equality, but in their hearts they are actually speaking with no fullness of meaning, for they lack respect for their black brothers. This lack is due primarily to their limited knowledge of what black people have contributed.

The Negro is not challenging basic American values. He wants to join the system, not upset it; he wants to come into the house, not bomb it, and he feels an inherent right to come in that house because he helped to build it.

The white American who moved into that house has no knowledge of black Americans having helped to build it. Martin Luther King wrote from his Birmingham jail that Negroes "are forever fighting a degenerating sense of 'nobodiness' and the issue is one of human as well as civil rights, and it involves mutual respect."

This respect is only possible when each values the comradeship, the cooperation, the help of the other. If the help, the cooperation, the work of the black man is submerged and is ignored, then we can never bring the light of reason and the good sense of humanity to bear upon the ignorance and prejudices that beget the hatred that afflicts our society today.

Finally, the United Nations General Assembly passed the Universal Declaration of Human Rights 20 years ago in 1948 and it said this basically: "to promote and encourage respect for human rights and fundamental freedoms for all without distinction of race, sex, language or religion."

This declaration was designed for the world, but I am certain it would apply to our Nation as well. I appreciate your joining with others at work to ease the torture which afflicts us by establishing this instrument that will do so much and encourage mutual respect for human rights and fundamental freedoms without distinction of race, sex, language or religion.

May I say finally in closing that I wouldn't want to give this committee any kind of direct instructions, but I would urge that if it is established, that it be careful about the kind of people that are selected to serve on the Committee. There are still so many millions in this country that would want to keep this information submerged.

I would like to submit to you one experience I had at a college last year. I spoke to 155 high school students who had been invited to the campus to hear me. I held up a $5 bill and I said, "I will give this to any youngster in this audience who will give me the first name, the last name, the year or the city in which it was invented."

Of the 155 youngsters present that night not one could claim the $5 bill. They were all black youngsters. You cannot charge it to them. Neither can you charge it to those who taught them, because the history books haven't carried that kind of information.

I will submit to questions if there are any. I say again, I repeat what I said before, that I hope that the Committee will recognize that there have been a number of efforts made in this regard to try to establish something. In most cases they haven't had the funds to work with or else they have been submerged by prejudiced leadership that didn't want to bring this information to the fore.

Dr. WRIGHT. Mal, you mentioned that there was apparently a negligence and distortion of the history of our people. How can you assure that this bill will not cement that kind of thing, based upon the activity of the Federal Government with respect to Afro-American affairs?

How do you know that giving the responsibility of this kind of thing into the hands of a Federal commission would not make it worse?

Mr. GOODE. I can't. I wish I could assure it. This is what troubles me in this overall thing.

Dr. WRIGHT. Can you think of anything in the history of the Government that would give you cause to believe that it might not happen?

Mr. SCHEUER. I can. I will suggest the President's Anti-Riot Commission Report of just a couple of weeks ago. That could have been a whitewash. That could have been a mealymouth report that said everything and said nothing.

It was a very hard hitting report that told it like it is. It is up to the Congress and the Administration to follow up that report and put meat on the skeleton. Whether they will do it or not, I don't know. We are hopeful that the Congress and the administration will follow up and put meat on that very terrific skeleton, but I think that everyone can say that that Commission, which was a federally appointed commission, really took a hard-nosed, courageous, and forthright view of the problem of the Negro in America.

It laid the responsibility squarely on the door of white America and placed the challenge where it beyongs—with the Congress and the President.

I have the same hope that if this bill is passed, the President will appoint a nonpartisan commission that has that same courage and hard intelligence and that that commission will issue the same kind of forthright report as did the Anti-Riot Commission.

Dr. WRIGHT. That report is already beginning to gather dust. It was almost a restatement made by a commission in 1922 in Chicago.

If you read the Wall Street Journal of March 1, it compares the findings of the Kerner Commission with the one in 1922. It is almost verbatim. People read these reports, and they file them away and then when they have another holocaust they write new commission reports.

The story of the Negro cannot wait for that. We have to have actions, not commissions.

Mr. SCHEUER. Congressman Gus Hawkins of Los Angeles.

Mr. HAWKINS. First I want to compliment you for what I think is a very excellent presentation. I think it is a strong articulate statement. It shows the necessity for a commission of this type.

I can understand, Mr. Goode, why ABC didn't recognize you in spite of your handicap, that is, being nonwhite, and certainly I want to commend you. I have just one slight comment.

I don't know whether one should comment on the views of a witness, not yourself, but the statement that Dr. Wright has mentioned about the hope of the Government not doing anything.

I share some of the reservations that I know he shares as well as you also, I am sure, Mr. Goode. I don't think any of us is so optimistic that we think that things are going to happen over night. I think that this is a very honest attempt.

I want to commend my colleague, Mr. Scheuer, for taking this position of being the initiator of this proposal. If the proposal doesn't do any more than what we are doing today—calling attention to the problem and getting views and getting them out into the open, so we can talk about the subject—I think through hearings, we bring out some of the facts that the Commission hopes it will eventually do. Even the statement that you have given to this committee today, which I think contains such excellent material, was material which was actually unknown.

You talk about the kids that couldn't claim $5. I would have been among them. I think that this is some advantage, whether we can persuade Congress to accept this bill or not. I think the great problem is getting Congress to act on anything.

It is going to be difficult to get a Congress that talks about austerity to create another commission. If anyone would like to defeat the proposal, that is one of the easiest things in the world to do. There are enough of us in Congress who, if the Commission ends up being a whitewash and not doing what we hope to do, we would be the first ones to really criticize it and to say that we had made a mistake and to try to do something else.

But to do nothing at this time is the greatest injury that one can do and I quite agree that the Commission on Civil Disorders is not going to collect dust, not in my area, because we have moved to implement it. We have had meetings with the city administration which is not a very liberal one, may I say.

We have already had the chief of police, who is also not a great hero of our particular area, actually come out in the open to tell us what he was going to do in the recruitment and promotion of Negro policemen in the minority areas as well as throughout the city.

I think that in some ways some action will come out of this Commission's report. I know the members of it. I know two members of it who are likely to be defeated perhaps in their own areas as a result of the courage that they had in signing this report.

When I listen to a chief of police from Atlanta take what I consider to be perhaps the most courageous stand and to say things that even we can't get the chief of police in Los Angeles to say, I say that this is some progress.

I am not so pessimistic that by just wearing down the forces of racism in this country, by proposing these ideas and trying them out, that we won't come up with something that I think may be useful.

Mr. Goode. I just want to add that I had an experience about 15 years ago at a Rotary Club where they had invited members of the Lions and Kiwanis Clubs and their wives. It was a large and exclusive district outside of Pittsburgh called Mount Lebanon.

I would only go during Brother Week when they invited me. I will never forget a very distinguished businessman, an executive of the Gulf Oil Corp., who said to me, "Mr. Goode, I have enjoyed what you said but I know I get tired of listening to Negroes demanding their rights. What contribution has your people ever made to this country?"

You could have heard a pin drop in the room until I picked it up and said, "That is a good question." I proceeded for about 15 minutes to cite case after case and then he stood up with tears in his eyes and his voice trembling and apologized.

The next week I had a meeting with him and then came the first selection of the first Negro girl in the Gulf Oil Corp. of America. You see the psychological advantage of this kind of thing and what Dr. Wright's group is doing and what Dr. Wesley's group is doing. I don't think we have to prove ourselves.

It is a damn shame that after 300 years we have to prove ourselves. But nevertheless it is there and it is staring us in the face every day.

I meet it in the city of New York. You come here and people tell you this is the greatest city in the world; this is the most liberal city in the world. I can't begin to tell you of the instances that I have experienced in the last 6 years that I have been here with ABC.

I am with ABC, so if I go around with a sign on my back, I am going to be treated like a special Negro. I don't want to be treated that way. I want you to make this a whole part of the record.

The introduction I didn't read will explain to you why I feel the way I do. I have six children and the oldest was awarded the Bronze Star. The second one, who is 27, is a graduate of West Virginia University. He is on loan to the Federal Government now by the Mellon Bank in Pittsburgh for the Plans-For-Progress Program.

The third one is a graduate of West Virginia University and is an employee of the State of Pennsylvania. Two are in college and I owe everybody. I say that because I want you to understand why I feel the way I do. This blackness is not something new with me, and I would join with whatever is proposed out of this group and I will hit the highways if necessary to help pass some kind of legislation that will get this thing out before the American public because, believe me, gentlemen, it is late; it is real, real late.

Mr. HAWKINS. I want it to be thoroughly understood that it has been said that this proposal should have been introduced by one of us. That is, by one of the Negroes in Congress.

Mr. SCHEUER. I would like to ask one question.

Do you come on the television screen for ABC?

Mr. GOODE. Yes.

Mr. SCHEUER. Then I would like to say that I can't imagine anything that would give young Negro children and young white children a better image of the Negro American and his participation in our cultural, economic, political, and artistic life than to have your face come on that screen and comment intelligently, articulately, and persuasively on American life and times.

That is the kind of breakthrough that we want to achieve. That is the kind of breakthrough that this Commission would be designed to achieve. If it can act as a change agent in opening up the doors to people like you to come into policymaking and executive-decisionmaking responsibilities, in our media, visibly so, then I think that we are well on our way of creating the kind of hero image, if you like, that both Negro Americans and young white Americans can enjoy and benefit from.

Mr. GOODE. That is a beautiful statement and this could cost me my job, but it doesn't make any difference. But I have a lot of rich friends like Dr. Wesley and Wright. It is nice of you to say that, but I would have all three of you in tears if I told you what these last years have been like, not only getting on but doing the thing that I am best capable of doing, because I am dealing with prejudice every day.

Everybody at ABC doesn't love me, and many people who work on ABC, no matter how Mr. Goldenson or Haggarty or the top executives I deal with or men down at the lower level, who are basically little white men, are people I must fight.

My problem is this, that my kids think I am the greatest guy that ever lived and that is basically all I am interested in, so I don't go running to Mr. Goldenson or Mr. Haggarty or anybody else. My father died in 1960. He was the son of slaves and the greatest man that ever lived, and when he died then I looked at myself. I had to protect myself.

But I lost thousands of dollars in income because of this. I think this is important because men like yourself who are out in the community and who are dealing with these problems seldom hear anyone tell you this part of it. They tell you this other part. It is like the city of New York. If the top of the fire department is a black man, then they think everything is rosy. If there are five Negro principals out of 168, they are saying—what is the Negro complaining about? I know five Negro principals out of all the principals in New York.

I cite this because I don't want to leave this table with a feeling of—it is nice of you and I feel honored for you and it has been said before. I think it is important that people in key positions like yourselves, you men who help to make the rules, to go behind the scenes to see what Bob Teague is up against in trying to stay on the air, and what a Joan Murray has to face at CBS, and what a Vic Miles in Pittsburgh has to face.

Mr. SCHEUER. I agree with that. Things aren't perfect. But I can't help recalling the words of a great philosopher who compared the act of a woman preaching with a dog dancing on its hind legs. He said the wonder of it is not that it is done well, but that it is done at all.

The fact is that you are a start and a great start, but if we can multiply you, then we can make that a great start. The fact is that you are here.

Ten years ago there was a testimonial dinner in my honor for work I had done in inter-group relations and housing. At the end of the dinner the head of one of the television networks came up to me and congratulated me. I said, "I appreciate those words and I hope I can congratulate you." I said, "I hope we can have a testimonial dinner in your honor some day." He said, "what do you mean?" I said, "when I see a black face on your TV network."

He said, "Could you help us find somebody?"

So immediately I got on the telephone and I telephoned Ralph Bunche, Bob Weaver, Roy Wilkins, and Whitney Young, and within a week one of them came up with a Negro American whose name would be known to everybody in this room, a superbly qualified individual who had an important position, but who thought this would be a great challenge. I submitted his résumé to this network. Several weeks went by, then a month and 2 months went by. And I was very embarrassed.

I finally called this executive and I said, "What's cooking on this fellow? Isn't he qualified?"

So the answer came back, "Jim, I am a little embarrassed to tell you this, but our top people think he is overqualified."

You are damned if you did and you are damned if you didn't. You are either under or overqualified.

The fact is that those doors have been thrust down a little bit, and your being where you are is evidence of it.

What we want to do is to create a commission that has representatives of the power structure in addition to representatives of great Negro scholarship who will act as change agents, who will have access to the levers of power, who will open those doors wider, who will multiply you by 10 or 100 times, who will enforce working conditions that won't subject future Mr. Goodes to some of the awkwardness and tensions and embarrassment that you have been subjected to.

I think you can take great pride that you have been one of the forerunners and pioneers that has seeded improved conditions.

Mr. GOODE. Let me say this, because I think you are a man of goodwill and good intent. I know men as powerful as you men are, and I have interviewed many of your colleagues—Senators and Governors and Presidents on three different times. But I think this business of the cracked door is not enough. I was 60 on the 13th of last month. How much more time do I have to go?

I don't want this thing for me to creep on forever. I worked for 12 years for the U.S. Steel Corp. and I never got a promotion. This is one example of things that are happening to thousands of black people around the country.

So, when you read about the dropouts and discouraged and hoodlum class, you find many of them with IQ's of 120 and 130. You can't keep banging your head against the wall and feeling that tomorrow is going to be a greater day.

My folks lived on that philosophy and that kind of religious faith, but the young black child in America today says, "Ugh, Ugh! I ain't going to buy that." But that is what kept us going up to the present time, that kept my father and my mother and my grandfather and grandmother in front of them, but this won't do in 1968. You need to pull the rug out from under the top people.

Congressman Scheuer, any top executive in America today would hand down the ruling, whether he is in ABC or NBC or the New York Times or wherever, that this is the way it will be.

I told you I am at the United Nations. We pay about 42 percent of the cost at the United Nations for its upkeep. There are 1,300 jobs at the United Nations that pay better than $15,000 a year. About 365 of them are held by Americans, and of the 365, nine of them are Negroes. This is what I am talking about—the overall thing.

Thank you for your time.

Mr. SCHEUER. We would now like to call to the stand a great American, Mr. Jackie Robinson.

Mr. Robinson, I would like to introduce you to my colleagues, Congressman Hawkins and Congressman Hathaway.

We are delighted that you came here today. Your statement will be printed in its entirety at this point in the record. You can either read it or, if you prefer, you can just talk to us, chat informally, and your remarks will appear after the printed version of the prepared text.

94-721 O—68——5

(The prepared statement follows:)

STATEMENT OF JACKIE ROBINSON, SPECIAL ASSISTANT TO GOVERNOR ROCKEFELLER OF THE STATE OF NEW YORK

I support vigorously the proposed legislation offered the House of Representatives by Congressman Scheuer and co-sponsored by his distinguished colleagues.

The bill at issue would provide for the establishment of a Commission on Negro History and Culture.

For many, many years, in these United States, a grave injustice has been done, not only to the Negro cause, but also to the cause of historical truth and accuracy.

We are all too familiar with the sins of commission which have afflicted black Americans—the sins of exploitation, of racial discrimination, of color prejudice.

Much has been written, said and legislated with regard to these inequities.

In my view, sins of omission which have victimized the Negro have been as hurting and as unfair as sins of commission.

One of the major sins of omission has been the failure of historians and educational authorities to assign to black Americans the credit they richly deserve for the collective and individual contributions they have made to American history and culture and to the growth of this country.

Textbooks used in America's schools have revealed that George Washington was the classic commander in American Revolutionary struggle, but failed to illuminate the fact that Crispus Attucks, a black free man, was the first American to give his life in that struggle when he fell mortally wounded in a skirmish with British soldiers on Boston Commons.

As children, we learned of a Longfellow and a Louisa May Alcott, but who revealed that black Phyllis Wheatley, a slave, and black Paul Lawrence Dunbar both wrote magnificent poetry.

Their works have survived in adult, classical literature, but the average American school child or older student is rarely advised that they existed.

Textbooks reveal scant information about George Washington Carver's agricultural discoveries, for which he refused to accept compensation and which fantastically enriched the entire American economy.

The discoveries and research of black physician, Charles Drew, concerning blood plasma-work which has saved the lives of untold thousands during World War II and subsequently is given little notice.

These are individual accomplishments.

On the collective front, one does not read of the black skilled and unskilled workers and artisans who during and after the days of slavery, built bridges and performed both simple and intricate tasks in engineering and construction.

Information is virtually invisible about the service and heroism and death of black Americans in every war in this Nation's history.

The lack of this information is psychologically crippling to every black child who attends our schools or uses our awesomely inadequate (in this respect) libraries.

His history, he is led to believe, is compounded of slavery, indolence after slavery, failure to contribute to and participate in the onward march of our Nation.

To deny him the material which refutes this is to deprive him of the sense of "some-bodiness" so necessary to every human.

To provide him with this material is to give him pride, incentive to accomplish and comfort in sharing this society with his fellows.

So much is said to indicate the necessity for change in the hearts of men and so little is done to implant in the minds of children information which could communicate intelligent responses to their hearts.

That is why enactment of this bill would be of such great import, not only to Negro children and students, but also to whites.

Before Mr. Branch Rickey enabled me to be the exponent of his noble experiment, whites in baseball could not truly claim superiority in the game.

For their competition had been only with whites.

Until white youngsters learn the truth about youngsters and the traditions of the Negro, they cannot lay claim to full education.

I like the proposed bill because it is specific and definite and, therefore, could efficiently accomplish its worthy aims.

It calls for Presidential designation of a commission of eleven authorities on Negro history and culture.

It seeks adequate staffing, unencumbered by normal qualification and salary standards.

It allows for consultation with and services of experts in various fields.

It proposes a study to create better understanding and knowledge of Negro tradition and contribution to America.

The bill suggests consideration of ways of discovering, preserving and collecting of materials not yet available; preservation and cataloging of such materials as are available.

The proposal for the establishment of a museum or Center of Negro History and Culture is dynamic in its potential.

Congressman Scheuer and those legislators who are associated with him in this proposal are to be highly commended.

In these days of racial crisis, a project to illuminate the background of the black American can only serve to help in unifying all of our people.

STATEMENT OF JACKIE ROBINSON

Mr. ROBINSON. I think that all of us have come here to support what you are trying to do to get this bill through and to let you know that we feel as strongly as I am sure that you feel and Mr. Goode felt when he finished his testimony here. I think he expressed his sentiments extremely well about what is going on.

One of the networks—probably the same network that you talked to—did attempt the same kind of thing you mentioned. They liked the idea until it got down to a certain point. We have been trying to get this gap closed for a long period of time.

If we can get Negro history, and if we can get different kinds of programs across, I think it's going to help a great deal.

As a matter of fact, a few weeks ago, the State Department of Education here in New York expressed an interest in a museum. They wanted our office and the State government to give them some help. They let us know that they have funds to move ahead in these areas, and they also have a building where they are looking to go into. I would think that if someone would talk to the State Department of Education and find out what they have done in terms of a museum for the Negro and to get Negro culture to the public, I think these things would help a great deal.

I think the interesting thing is that moneys they say we have will mean that perhaps the Federal Government doesn't have to involve themselves in providing moneys and getting this thing going, because this is probably the only reason that we are not going to move ahead.

I would certainly feel, as an individual coming before you gentlemen, that I support what you are trying to do. I think it's high time that the Congress understood the tremendous frustrations that the young Negro has today, frustrations I think we felt and participated in many years ago. That is the reason why we have so much concern for our young people.

Even though we understand the frustrations, we feel very strongly that we cannot condone the riots in the streets and these kinds of things, and we feel that a program such as you are starting here can help these youngsters to know that we care.

For too long we have been making promises, and our youngsters take a look at it, and for a while they believe, and then they don't believe. Unless we start taking the first steps and unless we start making a sincere program toward implementing some of the promises that we made, I feel that it's just not going to be enough.

We keep talking and worrying about 1967 and what happened. My view is that it was a little nothing compared to what 1968 will be unless the Congressmen, Senators, and the President of the United States recognize their responsibility.

We read now that the Congress is going to do everything they can to stifle the housing bill. Once again, it says to the young man: "You are not interested enough." And the youngster gets angry and then somebody has induced him, not because he wants to, but because the discouraging talk about these problems forces him to go into the streets.

People condemn the Negroes for boycotting the Olympic Games. We get a chairman of the U.S. Olympic Committee who adds to it by supporting South Africa's committee in the games.

I think you have a chance to do something, and I think that is why you are here. While I am frustrated and angry as everyone, there have been times when I felt like getting into the streets myself.

I conclude that if you can get a bill through which will provide the establishment of such a commission on Negro culture and get some more interest in the people, there is so much that can be done. Negro youngsters don't know about Dr. Charles Drew who gave us plasma. They can see Mal Goode on television, and it does help a great deal.

If we had something concrete supported by the Congress and supported by the Senate, it would be a sincere gesture that would get to these youngsters. These are the things that are going to be necessary.

We talk about Mal Goode and Roy Wilkins. The problem is that they, as individuals, have been able to achieve, but even they have not been able to point to things that they have been able to do to help others with less possibilities than they have.

What we need is to give the Mal Goodes a little more victory; give him a promotion.

I remember when they were looking for a guy to go on ABC. It was a tremendous thing to see them choose a man like Mal Goode. I knew him to be the fighter that he is. He won't say and do things simply because it is going to push Mal Goode. I think this is basically why so many of our youngsters are against people in responsible positions, because they feel that what they are doing is for individual gain.

I just want to congratulate you for what you are attempting to do, and I hope that we soon go forth. If we can get Negroes on this Commission, I am sure that they would be willing to stand up and be counted in important situations.

You might want to get down and get some of these youngsters off the street. Some of these black power guys who are on the fence are ready to fall either way. They speak awfully hard, but I think most of them are just looking for the opportunity of getting something, of being recognized for abilities.

Take the young fellow from CORE. You can't find a more militant individual from CORE. When one of the individuals got a promotion from a city job, he took it because he is looking for recognition. There is a tremendous amount of ability in these different kinds of organizations. If we can get them to understand that we do care, they might go into these jobs rather than go into these communities to stir up that trouble in the bottom of the cup.

I think you are on the right track. I hope that we can play a part in it. I don't know how, but I am sure it is possible.

When I came in here, I was quite pleased to see the caliber of witnesses. I knew you were inviting the right kind of people when I saw Mal Goode.

Mr. SCHEUER. We are delighted, indeed, that you came.

Mr. HAWKINS. I would be remiss if I didn't make reference to Mr. Robinson's former home. As a matter of fact, we are both graduates of UCLA, and I have a bone to pick with him in that I feel that we gave him a start and we regret that New York gained his leadership. I sometimes wonder just how we could have retained Jackie Robinson in Los Angeles.

Mr. ROBINSON. To me it's a very simple kind of thing. I think parts of Los Angeles, Calif., are worse than the South in terms of prejudice and discrimination. I think when California rejected the housing bill, their proposition 14, I believe, indicated to me that, while we were planning to move back to California, maybe this wasn't the right thing to do. Then, when I see them elect Ronald Reagan, this worries me, also.

I think just in terms of little things; I think I make my living easier here. I don't have any prejudices against California, but I think California has prejudice against me and other Negroes. This is basically why I am here.

Mr. HAWKINS. I am glad it's on the record, particularly about the new Governor there, as well as proposition 14.

Mr. ROBINSON. To me it is the prettiest State in this country. It's a hard thing to go to California and not stay there. If I could afford it, I certainly would do so.

Mr. HAWKINS. What you are saying is that if we can strengthen the Fair Housing Act and get rid of our Governor, you will come back?

Mr. ROBINSON. I had some arguments out there last week at the San Francisco Chamber of Commerce about your Governor. It seems that they don't like our Governor, but we don't like theirs. I would hope that Mr. Reagan and others who believe like he believes will truly understand the frustrations. I don't think they really understand them. I think this is why we are so opposed to Mr. Reagan, that he just does not understand what motivates the Negro today.

Mr. SCHEUER. You got a real education job to do out there.

Mr. ROBINSON. I don't think it's possible, because where at one point he has been a true liberal—so he claimed to have been at one time—he has gone as far to the right as he can, and I don't think he is coming back.

I like to see a man like President Johnson who was way over there, opposed to everything that was beneficial to the Negro. He saw the light and now in my view has proven to be the best President and friend that we have.

Mr. SCHEUER. You don't believe in the redemption of Senators?

Mr. ROBINSON. I do very much so. I don't believe that when a man sees the light and then goes back that it's kind of easy for him to change and go back. I just don't know about Mr. Reagan. He might be all right.

94-721 O—68——6

Mr. HAWKINS. I have enjoyed this. I did want to commend you on your excellent work, and I can say to the chairman of the committee, who is doing a terrific job in terms of this proposal, that I believe the comments of an individual who has gone through the struggle that you have gone through and has reference to our State, I know that it was a struggle, and I can see why you left. Certainly, your views, I think, mean a great deal to this committee, and I think certainly that your endorsement of this proposal will certainly be a tremendous help to this committee in selling this proposal across this country of ours.

I think that it's great to have an individual such as you, who has made a name in athletics, to exhibit such statesmanship in the public service field as you have done over the years, and I am proud of the fact that you come from our State.

Mr. ROBINSON. May I investigate this with our education department and contact you? Maybe there is some way that they can work with you or we can work with you. We will check it out, if it is all right, and see what we can work out together.

Mr. HATHAWAY. I enjoyed watching you in uniform. I wonder if you think that legislation such as this will help stem the animosity which we all feel has been brought about. In a way, Mr. Johnson is his own worst enemy. He has bent over backwards to help the black American. While helping the poverty program and other programs, he has built up this animosity in that he wants things done tomorrow. And now we are looking for ways to convince people that things just can't be done tomorrow.

Do you think legislation such as this indicates that Congress is trying to do something would help to stem that animosity?

Mr. ROBINSON. Yes, I think it can help, but I think also that you, those of you who believe as strongly as you do, are going to have to stand up strongly against the Melvin Lairds or the Gerald Fords. They may have the strength to do it, but I submit that responsible people who understand our democracy and what it means to black Americans, as well as white Americans, will also have to stand up to these guys who, in my opinion, are the worst enemies.

And I am sure that you will do it. But the problem is too frequently that your voices are not heard. I think very frequently that you are going to make your voices heard, rather than the Mel Lairds and the guys who are spreading the wrong kind of propaganda about the world. They don't talk about what you are doing here. This is what bothers me.

They are saying to the Lairds and these fellows that unless you are willing to work with this and give us the same things that are guaranteed in the Constitution, then we have to take whatever steps are necessary to get ahead. They point to the fact that last year they got more Congressmen and more Governors and mayors than ever before only because they went into the streets. If these guys will stand up again and try to deny us equal opportunity, you have got to expect some kind of action of this kind.

The Republicans will nominate a Richard Nixon who appeals to the backlash by saying that the people of America cannot expect progress until we get order. This is a lot of baloney. We have been sitting here patiently waiting for something to happen. This is the stupidity of the Republican Party. Negroes are going to give them less than the 6 percent they gave Goldwater. It's just a simple kind of thing; we are not looking at causes. All we are looking at is results and individuals and looking at groups of Negroes who get out in the streets and represent 3 or 4 percent of the entire population.

They don't care that the 97 percent is screaming for protection from even our own extremists. I hope that people will understand that while we are concerned and disturbed about what is going to happen, there isn't a single Negro leader in our country today who can get into the streets and prevent what we saw last year from happening. They just haven't had anything to present to these youngsters.

I think the Congress in many instances plays a role in getting these youngsters in the streets, and I think the report by the President's Commission on Riot Control put the blame on everybody. It didn't just say the Negro in the street was responsible, but they put the blame on everyone in our society.

Mr. HATHAWAY. I would hope that the image that Congress has is one in which the anthropomorphic monster won't prevail; that there are three people here who will continue to work. We hope that we can count on leaders like yourself to assure the people that just because their expectations weren't fulfilled today because we were outnumbered in Congress, doesn't mean that they are not going to be fulfilled eventually. Your leadership may help assure that people like Stokley Carmichael don't take over.

Mr. ROBINSON. Let's face it, the Negro isn't Stokley Carmichael. Even though we have people who support the Stokley Carmichaels and the Rap Browns, they are only a very small percentage, but unless something happens, that percentage can get bigger and bigger and bigger.

Mr. HATHAWAY. That goes back to our original question. Will this legislation be sufficient to stem animosity?

Mr. ROBINSON. It's going to help if we take that first step. If we recall back in 1954 when the Supreme Court decision was announced, the first thing said was that we understand the problems and what these things mean, and we are willing to move to help you to implement this by not demanding that it be done today. We said that we will undergo this step by step. They are still waiting for it to go step by step.

If you can take that sincere first step, and if you can let the people who are looking for this step know that it is sincere, I say, yes, it can help. They have heard this before, and it just hasn't worked. There haven't been enough of you to stand up.

Mr. HATHAWAY. We stand up and vote, but we are outnumbered.

Mr. HAWKINS. The gentleman from Maine, you weren't implying that there was any idea by the sponsors of this bill that this could be a substantial help in eliminating or preventing street disorders, were you? You said by passing such legislation, we would reach the problem that we were discussing.

Mr. HATHAWAY. I just asked Mr. Robinson if he thought that this legislation would help in some degree to stem the animosity.

Mr. HAWKINS. I know my sponsorship of it is not calculated to do this terrific job; that, I think, can only be done by a comprehensive program, including such measures as antipoverty and open housing.

I think this legislation is only a small part of that total program. Certainly I don't want anyone to get the impression that I feel that this legislation is suddenly going to solve any of these basic problems. I don't pretend to be offering this as a great antipoverty program, for example.

Mr. SCHEUER. I think we are all agreed that this program is just one small stone in a great mosaic that we had better paint pretty soon.

I think it was instructive to all of us. I am very pleased that you have participated in the higher education of at least one Republican Governor, and I suspect that other Republican Governors may be educated, too. I should say that in the interest of bipartisanship.

From your experience as a distinguished Negro American who made it to the top and who was exposed through all of our media as a great and noble hero to young Americans of all races, colors, and creeds, can you give us any insights as to how we can open up the door of the media, the radio, the press, television, to depict better and more broadly the contributions of great Negroes like yourself to American life?

Mr. ROBINSON. I don't know. It's a difficult thing. I think Mr. Goode expressed it extremely well. The problem once again, as I see it, is the people who run the media, not the President or the top men up there, but that little man down there in the personnel department or the general manager of the little station out some place that just won't play the Negroes on their program.

About 3 or 4 months ago Mr. Duckett and I felt that the real problem today is that the media is not doing enough. There is a chance to bridge the gap, if America truly understands what Negro America is all about.

We talked to a friend of ours who thought it was a very good idea. I couldn't care less who does it, but if on a daily basis we had people telling about the frustrations and what we want out of life and getting White America to participate, this gap could be bridged. Somebody telling it like it is, not telling it to please somebody else.

For some months we didn't hear anything. I think that basically the reason why they didn't go with me was that I supported the Negro boycott of the Olympic Games.

I was deeply impressed with the personal sacrifice of Tommy Smith, who said. "I would give my right arm for a gold medal." Yet a month later he said "I would sacrifice this if my refusing could help my people."

What they have to do is to take a look at all the kinds of things we are talking about here, understanding that we have got to get the ideas of the Negro across, understanding what makes a Tommy Smith frustrated.

But to answer your question, specifically, I think it just depends upon the individuals and what they want to do. It's not an easy kind of thing for anybody to go into private business and say, "You have to do this or you ought to do that." They will agree with you and when you walk out, they say the heck with you. When you come back, they always have some kind of excuse.

I don't really think there is an answer to what can be done to get the news media to come across unless we get to the sponsorship and unless the Negro himself understands his tremendous strength as far as his economic abilities are concerned. $30 billion is a lot of money.

If NBC does the best job, we are going to let it be known to CBS that NBC is a better sponsor. This is the role that we have to play. Along with white liberals we go, instead of breaking windows, to open doors. We have to use our economic and political strength to open these doors.

While we have gained some by the riots in the streets, these to me are victories that are not very lasting, and I think that we can gain strong victories by a unification of the Negro peoples along with liberal people who believe strongly. There are enough of them. I think in Cleveland and Gary the only way they won was because there was a coalition of Negro and white people working together.

If we get this going, I think you can see the breaking down process. Most of us say it's long range. I just can't say what is the best way to go about it, but something obviously has to be done and obviously it has to be done fast.

Mr. SCHEUER. Thank you very much for coming here. We are very grateful that you took the time to testify.

Mr. SCHEUER. We would like to call John W. Davis.

Do you have a prepared statement?

Mr. DAVIS. I have a prepared statement.

Mr. SCHEUER. Your prepared statement will be made a part of the record in its entirety at this point.

You can now briefly summarize your remarks and we will ask some questions.

(The statement of John W. Davis follows:)

STATEMENT OF JOHN W. DAVIS, SPECIAL DIRECTOR, DEPARTMENT OF TEACHER INFORMATION AND SECURITY, LEGAL DEFENSE AND EDUCATION FUND, ALSO DIRECTOR, HERBERT LEHMAN EDUCATION FUND, NAACP

Mr. Chairman and members of the Select Subcommittee, A Presidentially appointed Commission on Negro History and Culture as set forth in H.R. 12962 as introduced in the United States House of Representatives on September 18, 1967 by Congressman James H. Scheuer of New York and other distinguished Congressmen represents enlightened vision and high statesmanship. I am happy to testify in support of this proposed and long-needed legislation. Its possibilities for good are infinite as are its operational out-reach points to conscious appreciation and understanding in our Country. The promises of such a Commission would include practical and prophetic values for all of our citizens and our government as well.

I have some competence to testify on this subject of our concern. For more than 40 years I have advocated and worked actively for the improvement of Negro life and for programs of quality in the field of historical research as related to Negroes. My interest found expression through *The Association for the Study of Negro Life and History* whose founder was the late Dr. Carter G. Woodson. Dr. Woodson and I were friends and co-workers. His life was dedicated to the revelation of truth through research and the scientific documentation of the facts of Negro life to prevent the Negro from becoming a negligible factor in the history of mankind.

The objectives or purposes of The Association for the Study of Negro Life and History which was organized in Chicago on September 9, 1915 were:

1. To collect sociological and historical data
2. To publish books on Negro Life and History
3. To promote the study of the Negro through clubs and schools
4. To bring about harmony between the races by interpreting the one to the other.

Some of the well-known persons who worked with Dr. Woodson in the promotion of the work of The Negro History Association were: Raymond Pace Alexander, J. Rupert Picott, J. Reuben Sheeler, Oscar Smilock and Arthur B. Spingarn. Historians who have aided this work include: Ray A. Billington, Merle Curti,

Dwight L. Drumond, Clement Eaton, John Hope Franklin, Frank J. Klingberg, Benjamin Quarles, Arthur M. Schlesinger, Jr., Sir George Shepperson, Kenneth M. Stampp, Lorenzo D. Turner, Charles H. Wesley and C. Van Woodward.

Some of the accomplishments and achievements of The Association for the Study of Negro Life and History are:

1. Directing the attention of investigators to the neglected field of Negro Life, History and Culture.
2. Expanding the circulation of The Journal of Negro History and The Negro History Bulletin into South America, Europe, Asia and Africa.
3. Published 50 volumes of articles and documents revealing facts which were generally unknown.
4. Produced 29 monographs on Negro Life and History.
5. Organized and stimulated the historical and cultural studies of Negro Life by local clubs and classes which have done much to change the attitude of communities toward the Negro.
6. Collected thousands of valuable manuscripts on the Negro which have been made accessible to the public in the Library of Congress.
7. Encouraged the training of young men and women for research in the social sciences and for instruction in colleges and universities.
8. Published the first number of The Journal of Negro History on January 1, 1916 and since that date has published this scientific magazine regularly every quarter.
9. Originated the celebration of Negro History Week on February 7, 1926.
10. Brought out The Negro History Bulletin on October 1, 1937 and has published it monthly from October through June every year since that date.

Dr. Charles H. Wesley has continued the work of The Association for the Study of Negro Life and History since Dr. Woodson's death in 1950. Demands for authentic materials on the Negro in America increase daily. Even with the constantly growing numbers of scholars interested in writing in this field, the demands for scientific documentation of facts on the Negro cannot be met. In addition, no significant and agreeable center for the display of the valuable data on the Negro exists.

Unfinished business in the already projected study of Negro Life and History relates to: *The Negro in Africa, The Enslavement of The Negro, Patriarchal Slavery in America, Slavery and The Rights of Man, The Reaction Against the Negro, Slavery as an Economic Institution. The Free Negro in the United States, The Abolition Movement, The Colonization Projects, Slavery and the Constitution, The Negro in The Civil War, The Reconstruction and the Southern States, The Negro in Freedom, The Negro in Social Justice, The Negro in American Wars*, and, *The Contributions of the Negro to the Development of America.* More definitive and extensive work is needed in each one of these topic fields.

Study, documentation, research and publications are called for in many other areas of Negro Life and History. New respect for the Negro from his fellow countrymen and respect for himself will spring from more authentic studies and documentation of: *The Genius of The Negro*, Negro Voting in State and National Elections, The Negro in Literature and the Arts, in Athletics and Sports, in Music, in Labor, in Religion, in Government, in Church, in Inventions, in Creative Scholarship, in Agriculture, in Medicine, in Law and the Courts, in Public Affairs, in War and Peace, in Diplomatic Service, in Business, in the Professions, in Politics, in Positions of High Trust, in Diplomacy, in Journalism, in Education, in Activities of the Stage and Screen, in Population Mobility, in Rural Life, Negro Folk Songs, The Negro Family, The Negro in Private and Public Educational Institutions, The Negro as an American Citizen, The Negro Missionary, Negro Protest Movements, and, Negro Crime. These are subjects which are crying out for scholarly treatment and meaningful research.

The elimination of black Americans would call for the rewriting of American history. The presence of the Negro has been a shaping factor in American history and life. He is deeply embedded and involved in American culture.

The Negro is an integral part of the American biography. Fuller treatment of the stories of little used names of uncommon Negroes must be made to improve the image of the Negro himself and also enrich American life. Far too little has been written or said about: (1) James Beckwourth—the Negro who was made Chief of the Crow Indians and was called "Morning Star". He went West at 19, leaving a life of slavery; (2) George William Bush—one of the early American explorers of the Oregon territory; (3) Norbert Rillieux who invented the evaporating pan for sugar refining and thus revolutionized the sugar-refining industry; (4) Henry Blair, in Maryland—who patented a seed-planter for corn in 1834; (5) Henry Sigler of Galveston, Texas—who patented an improved fishhook; (6) Benjamin Bradley of Annapolis, Maryland—who constructed a working model of a steam engine—was given a place as a helper in the Department of Natural and Experimental Philosophy in the Naval Academy at Annapolis. His steam engine drove the first cutter of a sloop-of-war at the rate of 16 knots an hour; (7) James W. C. Pennington—who mastered Greek, Latin and German—received a Doctor of Divinity degree from Heidelberg University—and, wrote the first Negro History in 1841. (8) Paul Cuffe, Negro Merchant and Philanthropist, who learned navigation so that he could captain his Traveller to Africa and bring back to this Country African products which were needed by the American business men of his day and time (1811); (9) Henry E. Baker, Negro who, as Assistant Examiner of the United States Patent Office for many years, reported on 800 to 1200 patents that were taken out by men he identified as colored—before the year 1913. Our histories do not give full credit to these and other people of color. Their stories and the achievements of other Negroes await completion by research Scholars. White and Negro Citizens await them.

The story of Africa has to some degree been told and retold while for some reason the constructive works of American Negroes have been muted. Culture reflects the lives of people and their achievements and it is the function of history to present in truth the ingredients of Culture.

The legislation contemplated in H.R. 12962 now under consideration in the 90th Congress of the United States bespeaks the cultural self-interest of our National government and opens up channels for the free flow of constructive and purposeful ideas which are basic to harmonious community life and living. This legislation points to travel on the high road which leads to the realization of the freedom, peaceful pursuits and understanding inherit in the promises of the American dream.

The Commission, when approved by the Congress, would provide an inviting and adequate central facility from which information about Negro History, Life and Culture would be disseminated. Coordination and cooperation between this central facility and existing cultural organizations and institutions would offset duplication in work and programs. To facilitate the spread of knowledge in this important area mobile units might me used to reach people in rural or remote areas. In a word, a network of appropriate regional centers would aid the dissemination of information for utilization in the mainstream of American education and life.

The Commission's most important task would be to establish an instrumentality which would facilitate the destruction or elimination of harmful racial myths, to provide a bridge of understanding among groups through open communication on a high level, to open the windows of the Negro mind for the recognition and evaluation of a new image of himself, to set another standard for the evaluation of other human beings, and, to promote the general welfare of our Nation and its people.

I support the proposed legislation in H.R. 12962. I thank you for permitting me to make this statement.

STATEMENT OF JOHN W. DAVIS, LEGAL DEFENSE FUND, NAACP

Mr. DAVIS. I am happy to testify in support of this proposed and long needed legislation. I am sorry that I have got to scoot.

I want to call attention to two or three things mentioned this morning. One of them has to do with the matter of textbooks; 6,340,000 nonwhite youngsters use textbooks in which there is no reference to them whatever and think what that does psychologically to those children.

Most of those children are black children. I just left a conference on minorities and the textbooks. Its report is easily available to the members of this committee. The Department of Defense wanted 2 million copies of our manual to be used in connection with the training of soldiers.

In this conference in Durham, the day before yesterday, the publishers were present and they put up this plea—We are in the middle, we need some help.

They needed the help because we have this duel textbook system going on in this country. The textbook in the North has to be integrated or somewhat liberal. The textbook in the South is not saying anything about the Negro that is favorable. That is doing something not only to the Negro youngsters but that is doing something to the conscience of America and certainly to the black people in this country.

As you said this morning, it is a Civil War in the North, it is the War between the States in the South. All of this is language that anyone can interpret, and all of this is doing tremendous harm to this country. I am here supporting America. I am not here just supporting Negro people.

I am looking for America. The committee asked very legitimately about ways in which we can scatter this material. I hope your legislation will go through. I will do all I can to assist in that objective. We have got to spend some money and get the best brains in America.

Don't stop on white or black, but we have got to get the best brains in this country to get this material together so that it will solve part of the problem that we are up against.

There are many existing organizations that we can call upon to assist us in this. Some of this work can be started tomorrow. Some of it is going on now.

Dr. Wesley is handling the work for my old friend Dr. Wilson. It is a marvelous organization which I hope you will have time to talk about a little bit today. We need, in terms of a museum, something that is most attractive to people at home, to visitors to this country, to people who want some central place where they can go and get the exposure on this subject, not only for the betterment of people in America, but for an improved exposure abroad.

The organization that I am representing here, one of them, has been asked to set up a legal commission for the Indians. The Mexicans have asked us to put on a program for them. People are looking for relief, and this legislation that we are talking about here today can go a long way in providing ideas for people other than ourselves who need assistance along these lines.

Therefore, we need some facility that we can refer these people people to. This facility that we are talking about should not only be just a building in some central place, but you need decentralized structures that are in carefully chosen, carefully chosen areas. And then after we do that, we have got to have mobile units that will take the information out to the rural areas and out to the people who are remote from these centers.

This is a very important thing, so far as our Government is concerned.

This then, I hope, will help us in getting this business through. The curriculum has got to be reconstructed. Our education is not hitting the American need and group needs in this country. Our education, as a matter of fact, is encouraging people to get into the ghetto and to get into the streets.

We have got, then, to change the curriculum, if we want to get this into the main stream of American education and American life.

I think we need an entirely new set of guidance people in all of the schools of this country. A guidance teacher in Washington, D.C., to my knowledge, would see a young black boy coming in and that teacher in the past had known when the youngster put his face in the door that he was going into track 4. And when you get into track 4, you are off the track for anything in this country of a progressive sort.

I would say, then, that we need to make this, I repeat, that this Commission should be biracial. Separatism has no place in it. We don't want any more separatism. We have enough of that now.

I don't think we need Congressmen to worry about defining separatism and the rest of this thing. All we need to know is to work on facts that we have already. I would say that a strong biracial committee can do this thing.

I have put all of this down with something that Mal Goode has called attention to. I thought I would give you just two pages of uncommon Americans and what they have done.

There is a Negro down here in Maryland who developed our first steam engine. At Annapolis they put him in the Division of Natural and Experimental Philosophy. Then his invention was the first steam engine, driving something down the river at 16 knots. It was improved upon, but that was the beginning of it.

The sugar refining industry in this country comes from the pan that was invented and worked out by a Negro. We don't see any of that in the textbooks, and what I am arguing for now is this Commission's opportunity to change the image of the Negro in America.

He wants to respect himself and he wants other people to respect him.

Mr. HATHAWAY. I am convinced that perhaps the museum isn't the best vehicle to be used for disseminating this information.

Mr. DAVIS. I don't argue for a museum. I think if you want to put up something significant, that is a good thing. I would suggest that you take something that is in existence and incorporate this idea in it, with the understanding that it will carry out what we are talking about here today, and not just go along in doing whatever it is doing.

I don't want this to die by tying it into something that is existing now. This is too big an idea to tie it to some vehicle that is going in the direction and will sidetrack our interest.

Mr. HATHAWAY. Rather than a museum, perhaps we need a research institute to be supplying information that can be funneled into the school text.

Mr. DAVIS. I have mentioned that in the document. I mentioned the museum because in your legislation you mentioned the museum. I am simply saying that that is one thing you can do if you want to use it.

Mr. HATHAWAY. Thank you very much.

Mr. HAWKINS. The next witness is Dr. Wesley.

As a friend, I would like to welcome you to the committee. I am sure that what you say will have tremendous importance to this committee and certainly a great influence on the proposal that we are hearing today.

STATEMENT OF CHARLES WESLEY, EXECUTIVE DIRECTOR, ASSOCIATION FOR THE STUDY OF NEGRO LIFE AND HISTORY

Mr. WESLEY. Thank you, Congressman Hawkins.

I am Charles H. Wesley, the executive director for the Association for the Study of Negro Life and History.

I bring greetings to this committee from the association. Our organization is a grassroots organization scattered nationally throughout the country and has been in existence for about 52 years.

It was organized in Chicago in September in 1915 by five persons. It is an organization of historians, of publicists, of persons who are teaching history, persons who are writing.

We brought out the first issue of the Journal of Negro History, with which perhaps some of you are not acquainted, but that Journal came out in its first issue January 1916, which is 52 years ago. It hasn't missed a single quarterly issue since then.

But its subscription list has been very small. It has been around 5,000. We brought out also the monthly Negro History Bulletin in 1937. This is the 31st year of that bulletin. It runs from October to May and is used in the schools.

We have also brought out quite a number of books and monographs. For instance, we have that which we call *Four Steps for the School*, *A Child's Story of the Negro*, a volume on *Negro Makers of History* for the third and fourth grades, the *Story of the Negro Retold* for the upper grades, and then *The Negro in Our History*.

Upon that background, we support this bill. We support it with the approval of our national officers and our executive committee. The national officers include the man whose name was called this morning, John Hope Franklin, Benjamin Quarrels, both of whom have contributed more to the field of Negro history since Carter G. Woodson than most individuals who are members of our association.

Arthur Schlesinger, Jr., is on our executive council as was his father, Arthur Schlesinger.

When I say we approve this bill, there is more than my approval. It is the approval of the Association which approved it in connection with the correspondence which I carried on with them.

We are willing to cooperate in endeavoring to secure its adoption. We do it because for too long a period the history of the black people has been neglected and enough has been said to indicate that what we should be doing is collecting information, documents especially; documents are fundamental in the way of history.

It has been said—no documents, no history.

If we cannot collect these documents in some national way, then we are not going to have much history. This Commission can collect these documents, or can make the plans for its collection.

We in the Association have been endeavoring to do that and have touched, just scratched the surface so to speak, of this situation.

We, along with the Irish American Historical Association, the Jewish American Historical Association, the Catholic Historical Association, all sorts of ethnic organizations, including here in the United States the Russian Historical Association, all have been operating on the same basis upon which we have operated.

The fact that there has been a neglect is the fact which brings into existence the thought of this Commission.

Finally, why should the Federal Government be interested in such a program? One of the reasons why the Federal Government should be interested in it is because it will strengthen, it will develop the techniques for satisfaction to the dissatisfied peoples who are seeking equal opportunity and freedom of citizenship.

The Negro has been considered for too long a joke, a minstrel, a coward, a self-effacing inferior person, in the estimation of Americans. The Negro must be made into a man and a woman, a person and not a thing. History can do this. I am urging that it would be done and undertaken by this Commission.

Now the Government has done this before. A half century ago a Committee on the Documentary Historical Publications of the U.S. Government was appointed with a historian judge, Franklin Jamison, as the secretary of the Commission.

In 1950, President Harry S. Truman directed this Commission to make a report available showing the public and private writings of men whose contributions, as he said, in our history are inadequately published.

The result of this directive was a report to President Eisenhower on a national program for the publication of historical documents.

In 1958, President Eisenhower praised the Commission for its splendid progress toward enlarging the basic stock of source materials in American history. This Commission has bought up volumes of state papers published in documentary form, in book forms, and large volumes. Thus Congress has made commitments previously toward the appointment of a Commission.

Therefore, what is being requested is not an invasion, it is something that has been done previously. Finally, the duties of this Commission would be numerous ones. They would be, as I said, to collect documents, to make photo duplications of various materials, to make microfilm duplications and reproductions, to create guides and indexes and calendars of papers and union catalogs, and to deposit these in local archives, local libraries, local museums with local societies and local agencies.

This is needed in order that the public might come in contact with this type of information. Plans could be made to cooperate, therefore, with local, nongovernmental associations, with museums, with libraries, in collecting and preserving and actually publishing information which would contribute to an understanding and appreciation of the history of darker peoples in the United States.

In addition, there could be special advisory committees in a number of cities where efforts are being made now to collect information on the Negro. New York, Philadelphia, Chicago, Detroit, San Francisco, Atlanta, are areas where we have our branches and our clubs.

They started the idea of developing museums and agencies of various kinds without buildings. This is the type of thing which this committee could be doing, a part of which is explained in this document.

Mr. HATHAWAY. Don't you think we would be better advised to concentrate more on the media today and not the museum concept? Just as the theater used to be the place to go before the advent of television, the museum was the place to go before the more direct media were developed. It seems to me that we might be wasting a lot of our effort in concentrating on the museum concept, which is the concept where the individual has to go there to learn and he is used to having everything brought to him.

Mr. WESLEY. I agree. In fact, when a museum idea first occurred, I said, "Well, why can't we have a library museum, because libraries are useful institutions?" In museums people come in and look. Museums are interesting and valuable and do a great good in a number of areas. I don't know that the government should go into the area of an exclusive museum. You suggested that we could have the Library of Congress or the Smithsonian Institution do some of this museum idea.

I took up once, with the Director of the Smithsonian Institution, the question of doing something on the Negro as they were doing on the Indian. They set aside a little room about 16 feet by 12, something like that, where they said they would have a beginning.

Well, that is segregation, which we really did not want and we did not follow up on that at all. If we are going to have a museum that will be completely segregated and we are trying to get away from the segregation of persons at the same time, what is the need of segregating themes or materials? It seems to me that it should be and can be integrated under the tradition established by the Supreme Court in 1954 and made a part of the whole scheme of things.

That is my statement on museums.

Mr. HATHAWAY. You have mentioned a lot of books. Have those been introduced to any of the school systems?

Mr. WESLEY. They are used extensively. They are used here in New York City. They are in the libraries. In some cases they are in school libraries. Teachers own them and teachers use them. We have suggestions for teaching and using these books. We have guides for them. They are used in Detroit; they are used in Chicago.

One of the books has gone through 11 different editions because of the need for it and the wide distribution. We have done very well with these books. All three of them were initiated by Carter G. Woodson.

I have undertaken to expand them and to add to them, to add new materials as they have been brought up and discovered. We have annual conferences at Greensboro, N.C. Whenever we go into a city we talk with the people in the city about books and we have a conference on Saturday morning of that week and invite all the teachers in.

We have been to Los Angeles with several such conferences and we stir the city, so to speak, while we are there. There are white and Negro participants. For instance, there are more contributions by white authors to our Journal of Negro History than there are Negro authors, and that is because there has been more training given to whites in history who see this as a native field, a field that has not been explored. It is one of the easiest ways to get to a publication because the field hasn't been investigated very extensively and so a number write in it.

The same thing is true of our Negro History Bulletin. White people are interested. White historians are interested in this field. We have an integrated organization. I should say that there the differentiation was 50–50 when we held our last meeting.

We meet in October of this year at the New York Hilton, and we expect to have the same type of program that we had before. I think this association, among the smaller units in various areas of the cities and the offshoots of this association, still stands up as the standard historical association among Negroes in the United States and the world.

Our journal and bulletin go around the world, to India, to Africa. We are publishing next month in the bulletin an article by an African historian with a Ph. D. from Oxford on the scientific study of African history.

I hope I can send you copies of that, so that you can see the kind of journal which we bring out. But we need some help and we need this Commission. This association can go on as it is going on. We own our building, we have a small amount of money. We beg a lot of money. We make some money on books, and it goes back into the association. I myself am serving without salary. There are contributed services being given by nearly every person on our staff.

That kind of thing can go on for a long time, but it ought not to go on. We need help, and we believe this Commission can find the way. If it does more than issue a report, to which reference has been made, we will make it alive, because reports, as Congressman Hawkins said a moment ago, can cause action. If there is a report that is favorable toward the teaching of Negro history and Negro culture, action can follow.

Mr. HATHAWAY. I think it would be interesting if we got a list of such books and where these books are required reading. It would also be helpful if we could talk with the teachers.

Mr. WESLEY. California has approved teaching Negro history in schools. Connecticut and Michigan have approved the teaching of Negro history in schools, and our books are the main sources of history in the schools.

John Hope Franklin has published a "History From Slavery to Freedom." It is a history for high schools and colleges. Benjamin Quarrels has published likewise a number of things. They are both members of our association and got their start, were initiated, so to speak, by Carter G. Woodson, the founder of our association.

But our books are the major books that are depended on in the Nation for information about the Negro people.

Mr. HAWKINS. I want to recall the statement you made with reference to the association's contribution to the Los Angeles area. There certainly has been a tremendous influence, I think, in rediscovering, as it were, the history of the Negro and something about his culture.

I certainly want to commend the association for what it has done in the Los Angeles area, in particular, because I know about that.

There is only one question I want to ask. In a sense you have answered that question already. Do you feel that this Commission would stimulate local activity and private organizations and what is now being done already rather than in any way detract from it? You wouldn't look upon this Commission as in any way undoing what is now being done or discouraging local activity or in any way subtracting from some of the very fine things that are being done in many places?

Mr. WESLEY. I think it would be stimulating. I think it would be an advantage to have a statement, even though it is a report, from a commission which would give an impressive statement about the value of Negro history to white and colored people in the United States. It is the one way that the image of the Negro can be changed.

We used to think it would be changed by religion and by preaching and so on. That is out. What we need to do is to get it in the schools where a truthful image can be developed of this thing we call the Negro. Nobody knows what it is any more than they know what an Anglo-Saxon is or Jewish, if you will, or Irish.

All of these things, you see, need interpretation, and the Negro can have an interpretation. I do not believe as a person that any local museum or library would be injured by any action on the part of a commission, when the library and museum is doing a job of taking care of Negro history and Negro culture.

There is a Schomburg collection here in New York; there is a museum in Detroit. There is a museum in Chicago, and I believe the representatives of these are here. There is a museum in Washington, and foundations now and then give a nickel or a dime to these organizations.

I am not talking about Federal control, but I am talking about a commission to stimulate and to develop and stress the appreciation of the Nation for the Negro people. Just think how many, as someone said this morning, worked in slavery without pay and then were dumped and there began to be promises of 40 acres and a mule which never developed.

The Negro people have worked up from nothing and then someone wants to know why the Negro has to be helped when the other minorities, the Irish, and the Scots, and the Jews, and others, have established their own historical societies and have gone forward. They could do it because their people have been able to push forward and have been given the opportunities both of citizenship and the opportunities of employment.

Negroes have been the last hired and the first among those who have been fired almost all the time. We have got to change that, and we can change it by constructing the Negro into a person, into an American. Seventy-nine percent of the Negro people in the United States were born here in the United States. That isn't true of any other group. The others have been foreigners who have come in, second-, third-, and fourth-generation people who have taken over the Nation, so to speak, and put the Negroes over in the corner.

All we are asking in this bill is that the Commission give an opportunity for the Negro to occupy an equal place in history with the other peoples who have helped to develop this Nation, because America is ours.

Mr. HAWKINS. Thank you again, Doctor. It has been a delightful occasion.

The next witness is Dr. Charles Wright.

Dr. Wright, I don't know you personally, but through correspond ence, and many mutual friends, I have heard some wonderful things about you.

STATEMENT OF CHARLES H. WRIGHT, PRESIDENT, INTERNATIONAL AFRO-AMERICAN MUSEUM, INC.

Gentlemen, it is a privilege to have the opportunity to present before this assembly the views of the International Afro-American Museum, Inc., on H.R. 12962. The International Afro-American Museum, Inc., commonly known as IAM, is now three years old. We do not feel we exaggerated when we say that the experiences of these three years enable us to speak with some authority on those matters to which the Bill refers.

We, along with some of the other grass-roots organizations involved in the vital subject of the history of Afro-Americans, are opposed to H.R. 12962 on several grounds. Our reasons will be given below.

First, however, you should know something about the International Afro-American Museum, Inc. As a non-profit Michigan corporation that has gained tax-exempt status from the Federal Government, we currently have 1,400 members. Last year's income was more than $14,000. Our International Board of Directors includes representatives from the Bahamas, Denmark, Colombia, South America and Sierra Leone, West Africa.

The enclosed brochure lists many of the activities in which we are presently engaged. This list, we hope, will reflect the broad base of public support and involvement that are mandatory in ventures of this kind. Our experiences during the past three years have already accomplished many of the things that would be expected of the proposed Commission. And, we might add, at no cost to the Federal Government. This would appear, then, to make such a commission unnecessary. There are others who share our view.

Congressman Adam Clayton Powell opposed Mr. Scheuer's first proposal to establish a Negro History Commission (H.R. 10638) introduced in the House in August, 1965. Mr. Powell stated: "A race which denies its past has no future. Negroes deny their past when they remain psychologically incapable of coming together to erect a cultural monument to their racial heritage. Whether or not such a monument—a museum of Negro History—is constructed should depend on the Negroes themselves. The impetus must come from within the Negro community, not from outside it."

Congresswoman Francis Bolton Spoke in a similar vein: "A Negro Freedom Museum will be a very fine contribution. I agree with Dr. Wright that it should be developed by Negroes, themselves, rather than by the U.S. Government. To me, it would lose its basic point if the government got hold of it."

Both of these statements reflect an awareness of the drive for self-determination among Afro-Americans that will not be denied. Mr. Scheuer's H.R. 12962 ignores this drive and appears to collide with it.

The membership of IAM, as well as other similar organizations throughout the country, has clearly demonstrated the knowledge, skills and resourcefullness to do a creditable job in retelling our story. Support of these organizations could yield an even greater harvest of accomplishment. Our ultimate goal is to build a monument to the Afro-American's struggle for freedom, which will be in the form of a museum of Afro-American history and cultural center.

The bill placed before us for consideration does not represent a new idea. For many years the necessity for a Museum of Afro-American History has been felt and expressed in the black community. Likewise, commissions are no stranger to us. Those that are appointed to help improve the lot of the black man usually waste enormous amounts of time and money writing detailed reports that few people ever read before being filed away in the archives of forgotten documents.

The government—city, state, or federal—has clearly demonstrated its inability to deal objectively with matters involving the Afro-American. On the city level the fate of the Schomburg Collection is a case in point. The impediments that have scuttled the efforts of the civil rights and Housing Commissions are fairly typical of what happens to us when we are put at the disadvantage of the federal government. We must not allow this to happen in a matter so vital, so personal as our history.

One of the early architects of this bill was asked, "Can you assure us that a federally-sponsored museum project would deal fairly with DuBois, Garvey, Robeson and Malcolm X?" Of course not. The Smithsonian Institute, to name just one example, has been more concerned with reptiles and birds than with Black Americans.

Already the publicity created by H.R. 12962 has begun to diminish public support for grass-roots organizations such as ours. Some are raising the question as to the wisdom of supporting a private organization if the federal government is going to do it for us. What may be even more significant is the fact that we have not been able to induce a single black historian to state publicly that we exist.

The primary goal of this bill or any other Afro-American history project must be to instill in black people a sense of pride and a positive self-image, not to create archives, write books and build a museum. If this is to happen the people must be involved in every stage of the project. If pride and self-respect do not come from the efforts they will have failed, no matter how much money is spent.

The government, neither city, state, nor federal has ever shown itself capable of dealing objectively with any matter involving Afro-Americans. In our system such objectivity is impossible. Examples to the contrary are abundant. We plan to cite some of them during the Congressional hearings on H.R. 12962 in New York on March 18, 1968. While it is doubtful that we can influence those members of the Black Establishment who, almost to a man, are supporting Congressman Scheuer, we may be able to give our politicians an opportunity to weigh the implications of their present position. You, the public, can express your feelings in this matter by writing to your congressman.

Our recommendations to the Washington meeting were:

1. Assist in the immediate preparation of 100 Mobile Exhibits (similar to the IAM Exhibit). They would travel throughout the country, telling the story of Afro-Americans.

2. Assist in the establishment of a nation-wide system of Oral-History committees to record for posterity the wealth of stories that elderly Afro-Americans have to tell and, at the same time, seek out the many documents, artifacts, and so forth that are so necessary to tell our story.

3. Encourage and support grass-roots organizations that are already involved in Afro-American history. Some of these include: The Chicago African-American Museum of History and Art; The American Negro History Museum in Beacon Hill, Boston; and our International Afro-American Museum, Inc., Detroit. Other cities have similar groups in varying stages of development.

We offered our experience and assistance to the Washington meeting on February 15, 1968. It was pointed out that no act of Congress was necessary to get these programs started. Again, there was silence.

It is hoped that by the time of the hearings in New York on March 18, 1968 something meaningful can be started that will involve the people on a national scale.

Presents:

"HISTORY ON WHEELS"

African Art & History Exhibit

Photograph by James Boyce

AFRICA . . . . . .

The history of a continent whose peoples have a long and rich cultural heritage unfolds in the colorful exhibits of the I.A.M. Mobile Museum.

I.A.M. takes Africa's story to the public as it seeks to destroy the myth of Africa, a continent three times the size of the United States, as a land of jungles and savagery and no history. It aims to arouse the Afro-American's pride in his own past by telling the true stories of the historical and cultural accomplishments of Africa's people.

1549 WEST GRAND BOULEVARD
DETROIT, MICHIGAN 48208
TELEPHONE: 899–2576

94-721 O - 68 - 7

OUR PURPOSE

For over 300 years, RACISM -- the belief in the superiority of "White" men over all others -- has produced an American tragedy: the denial of the historical identity and heritage of Africans and their Afro-American descendants. Most of our nation's history books and museums have ignored the Black man's past. The many contributions of African peoples to the development of the American nations have gone unknown and unacknowledged.

WE ARE NOW INVOLVED IN A REVOLUTIONARY MOVEMENT THAT WILL HELP TO FREE MANKIND FROM THE BONDS OF RACISM, AND ESTABLISH ONCE AND FOR ALL THE ESSENTIAL EQUALITY OF ALL MEN. THIS IS AN IMPORTANT AND DRAMATIC EVENT IN HUMAN HISTORY AND THE WORLD NEEDS A PERMANENT, INTERNATIONAL MONUMENT AS A LIVING SYMBOL OF THIS STRUGGLE.

The members of I.A.M. believe that no better monument can be devised than a magnificent museum devoted to telling the stories of Black men in history.

Although the museum will be primarily concerned with the contributions and achievements of Black peoples in the Amecas, its displays will also focus attention on the African past, the truth of which has been denied to us. We believe that knowledge of the past will help to give an accurate sense of the Afro-American's identity and worth to all peoples. Knowledge is power; and this kind of power will free the minds of Black men . . . and White . . . from the tragic distortions of RACISM.

I.A.M. dedicates itself to a single theme: that generations of Black children to come will be aware of and take pride in the history of their ancestors and their magnificent struggle for freedom.

FROM 1965 UNTIL NOW

From its inception on March 10, 1965, when a group of thirty-three citizens met to seek ways of erasing the distorted image of Black people in America, I.A.M. membership has grown to over 1500. In these three years, I.A.M. has produced a play, weekly radio programs, developed on oral history program, and lecture series, and began the publication of a newsletter. The mobile exhibit, I.A.M.'s major credit to date, was open to the public at the Michigan State Fair in August, 1967.

ON–GOING I.A.M. PROGRAMS

–Weekly radio programs broadcast on Saturdays at 7:30 p.m. on WJLB, 1400 KCS, in Detroit.

–Development of a library of oral interviews on tape which tell the personal stories of elderly citizens who have lived through much of the struggle for freedom.

–Lectures by our speaker's bureau, and a lecture series on the history of African and Afro–American peoples.

–Newsletter published quarterly and containing items of historical interest.

–Future publication of daily memorandum books with events in the history of Black peoples for every day in the year.

–Future production of place mats to be sold in public places. Each mat will present stories from Afro–American history.

–Production of a 15–minute film on Black men and women in medicine and other disciplines.

All programs are designed to uncover and present historical facts for the general education of the public.

SUPPORT

I.A.M. is a unique grass-roots project. It depends for its major support on the contributions and voluntary work of a lot of dedicated people. The mobile exhibit was prepared entirely by voluntary labor and the gifts of some materials. In addition, I.A.M. has had financial support from the Michigan Council for the Arts, the Detroit Public School System, as well as church, fraternal and private social organizations. The Detroit Historical Museum provided facilities for the preparation of the exhibits.

YOU, TOO, MAY HELP.

Your membership with the International Afro–American Museum will support the programs of I.A.M. and help build the permanent museum.

I.A.M. is a tax exempt, non-profit organization.

WHO MAY JOIN?

All persons concerned with human freedom.

WHY JOIN?

To demonstrate your personal conviction that Afro–Americans are a people of worth and dignity.

WHAT ARE THE BENEFITS?

The knowledge that you are sharing in the struggle for human dignity and freedom. Members receive the I.A.M. Newsletter, periodic reports, invitations to general meetings and the chance to DO rather than merely SAY.

INTERESTED?

There is a membership designed for every individual or organization. By completing the membership form below, you, too, will some day say, *"I helped build that Museum!"*

CUT ON LINES

SELECT ONE:

Youth (under 18) . .	$ .50	Sustaining	$ 25.00
General	2.00	Sponsor	100.00
Active	5.00	Benefactor	500.00
Contributing	10.00	Organization and up	25.00

Name ____________________

Address ____________________

City __________ State __________ Zip ______

Return to:

International Afro–American Museum, Inc.
1549 West Grand Boulevard
Detroit, Michigan 48208

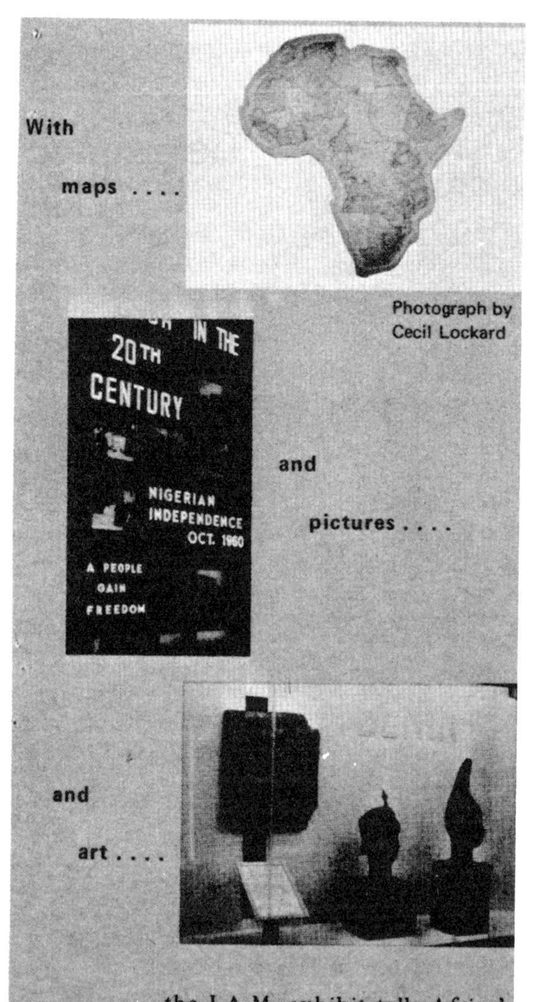

Photograph by Cecil Lockard

. . . . . the I.A.M. exhibit tells Africa's story from the origin of man, 2,000,000 years ago, to the emergence from colonial rule of free nations in the 20th century. Most of the known major developments of this long time span are depicted.

AFRICA LIVES! . . . . . with the early farmers of the Sahara, the colorful and talented peoples of the Nile, the traders and metal-workers of Kush, the sea-farers and merchants of Mombasa, the builders of Zimbabwe, the camel traders of the north, the gold and grandeur of the Empires of Ghana, Mali and Songhai, the skilled craftsmen of Benin, Oyo, and Ife, the rich and powerful kingdoms of Dahomey, Ashanti and BaKongo.

It is a pleasure to meet you and I know you will have a provocative but a very constructive statement. Without objection your statement will be entered at this point and you may summarize from the statement.

(The statement referred to follows:)

STATEMENT OF DR. CHARLES WRIGHT, PRESIDENT, INTERNATIONAL AFRO-AMERICAN MUSEUM, INC., DETROIT MICH.

Mr. WRIGHT. I am Dr. Charles H. Wright and I am here to speak in behalf of that organization plus some other grassroots organizations around the country, one of which is represented by Mr. Charles G. Burroughs of the Chicago Museum of Arts and History.

Our position is more or less the same. We would like to hold up for recognition many of the things that are happening in the country, the black communities throughout the land that apparently are not well-known. And they would tend to make such a commission as this unnecessary.

The activities that these organizations are engaged in encompass many of the things that the museum purports to do and they are being done at no cost to the taxpayer. What is even more important, they involve the will of the people.

For instance, our museum group in Detroit represents 1,500 people, mostly in Detroit, but through the nation generally. We are now 3 years old. We have engaged in a great variety of activities. We have answered many of the questions that are being asked in this bill to the satisfaction of the people.

We think that the purpose of a venture like this is not primarily to build a museum or to establish a Commission, but to rescue 25 million people from the position of being unpersonal things. This can only happen if the people are a part of the action from the very beginning.

This is why a grassroots organization like ours, like the one in Chicago and like the one in Boston, just to mention three, are most important areas for beginning this kind of consideration rather than from above downward. It is not just our objections that I would like to register, but those of Congressman John Conyers, who stated our position, exactly in his letter of March 6 to me.

There is also a letter from Congresswoman Frances Bolton, who stated, "I heartily agree with you that if there is to be a history museum, it must come from the Negro peoples themselves. Perhaps the manifestation of this merit as human beings will give them the pride and sense of worth of which you speak."

Congressman Adam Powell wrote in 1965, "The impetus for such a museum must come from within the Negro community and not outside of it."

We know that there are the resources available in the Negro community to do this kind of job with the support coming from the outside to stimulate the resources that are therein.

According to what our experience has been recently with commissions, one of the last things we need today is another commission. Our files are replete with congressional commissions that have cost enormous sums of money and consumed enormous amounts of time, writing investigative reports that have not nearly yielded the results that were intended.

Since this bill was introduced in 1965, I do note that there has been a hiatus of activity in some areas that would have been going along waiting for this bill to come alive.

Mr. SCHEUER. This bill was introduced for the first time in 1967. It is not comparable to any bill that was introduced before that. This bill is not to establish a Negro museum. This bill is to establish a Presidential Commission which would investigate the entire range of Negro history and culture in our education systems, in our textbooks, radio, TV, the press and which would devise a comprehensive program of collecting and disseminating the materials on the contributions of Negroes.

I refer to H.R. 10368 that was introduced in 1965, in August, and that is not the bill that we are considering now.

Mr. WRIGHT. I am saying that that bill related to the same thing.

Mr. SCHEUER. It is not the bill we are considering now.

Mr. WRIGHT. The history dates back that far.

Mr. SCHEUER. As a matter of fact, I was the sponsor of that bill that you mention. The reason that I put in the current bill was because I respected criticism like yours that we shouldn't concentrate on a bill to establish a Negro museum, that this might well be done better by the Negro community and there were others who echoed the views that you are giving us now. They recommended that we broaden our sights and consider the whole range of the media in America—press, radio, television, our education system, our teaching curriculum, our textbooks and that we come up with a comprehensive program about how the contributions of Negroes in America could be disseminated more forcefully through all the media.

It might well be that the Commission would come up with a plan to fortify existing institutions, just as you have suggested, and not to create a separate Negro museum.

That again would only be a small part of the many areas to be considered by the Commission.

Mr. WRIGHT. The bill does not in my view give an opportunity for the will of the people to express itself or observe any meaningful interest in its deliberations. It does detract from the community.

In Detroit we have had some people who indicated an interest in supporting this. When they find out Washington is getting ready to do this for us, they say we don't need your organization any more. Some of the educators around the country that we have asked to stand up and support our organization or be counted in terms of giving us publicity generally have stated that they are concerned about what is happening in Washington.

In other words, there is a polarization, and we say that this tends to undercut the community action and this is a private, personal affair involving black people.

Whether this committee realizes it or not, there is a new mood in the black communities. One, of self-determination and self-expression and this mood must be heard and dealt with. This is what Congressman Powell meant when he said that the initiative should come from within the community and not from outside of it.

The organizations and movements that take into recognition these forces that say that we are now able to speak for ourselves and demand the right to do so are more likely to succeed than those who tend to ignore it.

My recommendations were made in Washington last month and are reiterated here. They include assisting in the immediate preparation of 100 mobile exhibits similar to the one that we have prepared in Detroit. I have posters showing a mobile exhibit that we prepared in Detroit that has traveled throughout the city and the State and has been seen by 75,000 people and is now under contract with the Board of Education. This was prepared by the people at a cost of some $6,000 to $7,000 and it has created such an impact in the Detroit area that the metropolitan fund is considering outfitting three more for this summer alone.

This is just one of our programs. Another committee goes to take tape recorders into their homes of elderly Negro citizens and tapes their stories. We have found documents and photographs that are important in our history. This is one way of collecting our materials.

We have a radio program that helps us disseminate our material. These are happening daily in Detroit and could be happening in 100 communities with the proper support. These things are not costing the taxpayer one dime and do not have to wait upon the deliberations of a Congress.

As someone has indicated before, the time is running out, and in Detroit we have involvement. The second is to assist in the establishment of oral history commission to record for posterity the wealth of stories that elderly Afro-Americans have to tell, and at the same time seek out the documents and artifacts that are so necessary to tell our story.

Third, to urge current organizations that are already involved in Afro-American history, such as the Chicago Afro-American Society of Negroes and art.

This does not exhaust the list. There are others that are germinating with very good resources in the community. We think it is important to bring the material to the people, and the mobile exhibit is just one of the ways that we have found very effective in doing it.

I know it is late and I am sure you have some questions which might bring out some important points that I have not touched.

Mr. SCHEUER. We very much appreciate your coming in from Detroit to speak to us, Dr. Wright, and you have certainly given us a good deal of food for thought.

Mr. HAWKINS. I appreciate your frank views, although I disagree with them. There are several points, it seems to me, that have been overlooked. One is that today we don't have a national commitment as such for such studies to go on. It seems to me that this would greatly stimulate activity if the Federal Government were to give a national commitment in this field.

Secondly, you speak of grassroots efforts and the voluntary efforts. Perhaps in Detroit you may have a very excellent program. From what I understand you do, and I know that in some other places great efforts are now being put forth. But in some places I know there is absolutely none.

You see, I am worried about the many areas in which there is practically no activity at the present time. As to the argument that this should come from the people, I don't know where Mr. Scheuer got his ideas from; I don't know whether he just dreamed them up one night in his sleep, but I know the people in my area.

Mr. SCHEUER. I got ideas like this by talking to insightful people like you.

Mr. HAWKINS. I have gotten my ideas from talking to people in the street.

In connection with these I have had occasion in the past weeks since I knew about the introduction of this bill to discuss it with many people. I don't know what we call people in the streets—grassroots perhaps.

I have received absolutely no opposition at all. Just the opposite from people in Los Angeles and some of the groups there; the present groups that are studying Negro history in an organized fashion think that this would be a great help to them.

The antipoverty bill did not originate with the poor, but it certainly is helping reach the problem in a small way, at least. It seems to me that when you talk about the expressions of the people that all we can say is that those who are elected by a certain number of people to represent them speak possibly as much for the people as anyone else, and I just think that as an elected officials, I must speak for some of the people in my area. And, as I say, I have not heard any of the arguments that you have raised from the people in my area.

Dr. Goodlett is very critical and did communicate his views to me and I haven't had a chance to discuss them with him. I can't see how this bill would undercut what you are doing. If it did, I certainly would not be supporting it.

Mr. WRIGHT. I explained to you how it has already begun to do so. People are so accustomed to the Great White Federal Father with the usual paternalism doing things for us. When they find this is likely to happen, they are prepared to wait and see if it does.

If we are every going to arrive at a status of pride and maturity, we are not going to wait for the Federal Government. You speak about Federal commitments. The Federal Government has committted large sums of money to the Smithsonian Institution.

I went there one day and I was furious when I left as to how shabbily they had treated black Americans and I talked to several other travelers from other States. To a man they were furious, and I sat down and wrote to the Smithsonian and asked them how could they manage to mistreat the black Americans.

We know what is happening to the Schomburg Collection. You see, to sit here and talk about what should happen is one thing.

Mr. HAWKINS. The Smithsonian Institution is not a commitment in this particular field. I think this bill zeroes in on it and specifies it and it seems to me that would be a commitment.

Mr. WRIGHT. You mean it would be handled by a different form of government with a different result.

Mr. HAWKINS. I think in a sense you are assuming the bill does more than what it really does. The bill as I read it only sets up a commission to explore these various things.

Now this commission might easily conclude that nothing should be done. It might conclude that such local efforts as you have indicated are best. Certainly this is the easiest thing to sell in Washington. We have had no problem selling your idea.

Mr. WRIGHT. We don't need a commission to do that.

Mr. HAWKINS. There are people who do.

Mr. WRIGHT. I don't.

Mr. HAWKINS. You differ from others. You are not speaking for every person who has an interest in Negro history and culture. There are some who do belive that and there is an effort now to resolve this conflict. To resolve it, it seems to me, we should decide whether or not some organized effort on a national basis is needed or is unnecessary so that we can put to rest some of these fears.

I don't know any other way you can do it. You certainly can't go out and take a poll. I don't know how satisfactory that would be.

Who is going to underwrite it? I think that what you are suggesting is, one, that we shouldn't do anything or, secondly, that we shouldn't use taxpayers' money for this purpose.

I am sure that Southerners in Congress would be willing to endorse your idea 100 percent.

Mr. WRIGHT. I have not said that. I said activity does not cost the taxpayers money. I have recommended supporting the existing organizations.

Mr. HAWKINS. By taxpayers' money?

Mr. WRIGHT. Yes. You made a statement that there were not other activities; you infer that what is happening in Detroit, Boston, and Chicago is unique. What you don't realize is that we have a great deal of trouble getting publicity for what we are doing.

Mr. Scheuer had not even heard of us when the February meeting was programed. None of the organizations were listed on his program so we would come and tell him what we are doing.

Mr. HAWKINS. The bill accomplished something already then, hasn't it? He didn't know about you and I didn't know about your operation.

Mr. WRIGHT. It was through my efforts that I got on the bill. It was at my expense that I came to Washington.

I was sort of at the tail end after insisting that I have a chance to say something.

Mr. SCHEUER. We were happy to have you participate in that conference.

Mr. WRIGHT. I appreciate that. When you can deal in this field for 3 years since 1965 and still not know about us, with an organization of 1,500 people and doing the kind of thing we are doing, you are on thin ice when you say that there aren't other things happening.

Mr. HAWKINS. I didn't say there weren't other things happening, but there are over 20 million Negroes in America. I would say that if those 20 million know of your efforts I would be terribly surprised. And this is not to downgrade what you are doing, I would say that if a million know what you are doing I would be surprised, sir.

Mr. WRIGHT. There are not that many.

Mr. HAWKINS. My point is that there are 19 million other Negroes, minus those who might have similar efforts such as yourself, who are not being served. Perhaps in some areas an excellent job is being done.

I don't think that any one of us can say that an adequate job is being done.

Are you suggesting that we should amend this bill or change the idea to set up a grant and aid program so that the Federal Government would underwrite local effort throughout the country?

Mr. WRIGHT. Find the money in whatever way you can, immediately, so we can expand the programs that are now in existence. Because commissions take a lot of time and money and you don't always get the proper results you want, and when you get them people don't act on them.

Mr. HAWKINS. Who would administer that grant and aid program?

Mr. WRIGHT. This could be decided by the people.

Mr. HAWKINS. By what people?

Mr. WRIGHT. The people who are concerned with the whole history movement. There are a lot of us throughout the country.

Mr. HAWKINS. I don't see how you can put your ideas and suggestions into operation except through elected officials. They are the ones who are going to vote on the association. They are the ones who are going to set up the agency for this grant and aid program. That is going to be handled by the people through the elected representatives.

I don't know what group of people you are going to call together and have decided how they are going to spend Federal money. If so, this would be a very innovative process in our Government.

Mr. WRIGHT. It is not novel. People are writing programs that are being funded by the Government every day.

Mr. HAWKINS. It is an idea that may originate with the people, but doesn't it go to some formal Government agency, some bureaucracy in Washington that decides whether there is an authority for the expenditure and there is a committee that decides whether it should be done?

Mr. WRIGHT. One of the programs that our mobile exhibit had a contract with were the board of education. It ran 50 days with the rental of $100 per day for this exhibit to take to 13 high schools, 1 week each. This money came from cultural money which was Federal Government money, but we wrote the program.

You see, it came through HEW or one of the other organizations. It was Federal money.

Mr. HAWKINS. Do you feel that if your idea has the backing that you apparently think it does, and I am sure that it does have substantial backing, that you could convince the Commission that this is the way it should be done? Because unless we have some representative group making a strong recommendation to the Congress, I don't see anything happening.

Mr. WRIGHT. What commission are you referring to?

Mr. HAWKINS. The commission that would be created under the terms of this proposal.

Mr. WRIGHT. I hadn't figured on dealing with that commission. I went to the Association for the Study of Negro Life and History because, as Dr. Wesley said, it is the oldest and most respected organization in this area, in 1965 and presented a proposal to them that we generate increased activity, and told them what we were planning to do.

This is the kind of agency that I can see that could expand its broad span of action and include a greater variety of activities that are now being accomplished. There are organizations to carry on these functions.

Mr. HAWKINS. I am sure that many changes can be made in this proposal and I am sure that Mr. Scheuer has been in public life long enough to know that you must be flexible. And I just think that dedicated and sincere people, such as yourself and the members of this committee, certainly should be able to find a common ground.

I would hope that something be worked out so that we do have the support of individuals such as yourself and those whom you represent, because I think we are seeking the same thing. I just think there is a misunderstanding and I don't blame you for being very suspicious.

Mr. WRIGHT. Is the Federal Government able to deal objectively with any matters dealing with Afro-Americans? There are a lot of people who feel suspicious.

Mr. HAWKINS. You are suggesting that you are going to deal with the Federal Government. It would be all right that the Federal Government subsidize this?

Mr. WRIGHT. On our terms.

Mr. HAWKINS. The Federal Government doesn't always deal with individuals in the field. I think that some criteria or standard certainly should be worked out and I don't think this has any reference to black or white or any ethnic group. I think that all of us subscribe to certain standards in education and in all of our institutions and I am quite sure that some standards are going to be required.

The Federal Government isn't going to go out and say, "You are the grassroots and you want some money, we are going to give it to you."

Mr. WRIGHT. I think you are oversimplifying it. I only came to demonstrate what a group of citizens in Detroit have been able to do in 3 years. We have a history of involvement, we have a history of successes in several areas involving Negro history.

We feel that this is a prototype of what is happening in Chicago and Boston and what can happen in many areas. We are suspicious of the heavy hand of the Federal Government getting involved. This has already demonstrated to us that it is having a negative effect on what we are doing.

Mr. HAWKINS. I certainly would hope that this committee, and if not the committee, I personally say to you that I will come out to Detroit and see what you are doing because I would like to know what you are doing. I hope it would be the committee, but if not the committee—because we are limited also as to getting money from the Federal Government—I certainly make a promise to you that I personally am interested in what you are doing, and I will make a trip out there very soon.

I certainly enjoyed this opportunity to discuss the matter with you.

Mr. HATHAWAY. Thank you, Dr. Wright, for testifying. I certainly appreciate your concern about someone taking the initiative in these matters. I can assure you that we will make some effort at least to incorporate your idea into what we have outlined in this bill.

As you know, this isn't the final product. We do spend considerable time remodeling it and redrafting it based upon the hearings that we have had.

I would like to ask you one question with respect to your dissemination of information. I understand you have three ways. Have you attempted to do anything in terms of television or radio?

Mr. WRIGHT. We have a weekly radio program that is one half-hour every Saturday at 7:30, and this program was given to us as a public service by the station. We are at liberty to use it in whatever way we see fit. We use the program to, of course, tell about our activities. We interview important people who are in town and we hold up to view important Afro-Americans.

The program coming up this Saturday will deal entirely with Mr. Tolson who is one of our great poets, who died about a year ago. We are doing an entire program on DuBois. I was just appointed the chairman on the board of trustees of the education TV station in Detroit last month, and I was appointed because of my relationship with this organization. They are going to do more programing in the area of Negro history, and they felt that I could feed in this kind of material to them.

We have a lecture series tonight. Mr. Otis Smith, who was formerly our supreme court justice, is going to talk about reconstruction politics. It's a 10-week series. We have 10 lecturers, one each Monday night, and we are taping these lectures, and we are going to put them on the air. We are going to feed them in, transcribe them when we get the money, and put it into a pamphlet to be disseminated.

Last year we had a course on African history that was taped, and I have a copy of one of the lectures. I was taking it to the station that wants to review it to bring the series to the New York area.

Mr. HATHAWAY. Have you had a chance to evaluate the effect of the program?

Mr. WRIGHT. They are not as effective as they should be because they are not given the full-range radio and broadcast media. Despite the fact that we were at the state fair where we saw 16,000 and despite the fact that we had been to thirteen high schools, Detroit television media had not considered us because we are black. We are not saying we hate anybody. This is what a Negro must do to get on TV.

This answers your question that you asked Jackie Robinson. We can't do anything unless we get white leadership, which I object to. After we got downtown and the new Detroit committee decided that we had some kind of rating, then the media came in and did a 3- or 5-minute thing on us. The city as a whole began to see that we existed, and now our effectiveness has improved.

Mr. HATHAWAY. How about educational opportunities?

Mr. WRIGHT. We are in the Detroit schools in one capacity or another all the time. When I get back Thursday night, I have a session with the teachers and the people and the parents in one of the PTA groups because our van is coming to that junior high school.

Before the van comes, we send in a team to do a preparedness program involving the teachers and the program, and then we send a taped message, and we send them materials that we have printed.

In this way we are trying to saturate the area and do a job that way. We are limited by funds, and we have a lot of volunteer people.

Mr. HATHAWAY. Thank you very much.

Mr. SCHEUER. Dr. Wright, I have enjoyed your testimony enormously, and I think you have done what is apparently a remarkable job in Detroit.

What puzzles me is why you, of all people, should be objecting to this bill. What this bill would do, among other things, is to create a medium, an engine, through which the breakthroughs that you have accomplished in Detroit could become widespread. Look at your access to education television since you are on the board of the education TV station. You are now a mover. You are a decisionmaker. You have managed to penetrate the schools, the education system. You have got a regular sustaining radio spot. In effect, you have made it in Detroit, right?

Mr. WRIGHT. No, I haven't. You want things in neat little packages, and they are not that way. You have no background. I haven't made it in Detroit.

Mr. SCHEUER. You have made a breakthrough?

Mr. WRIGHT. I got one big toe in the door, and that can close tomorrow.

Mr. SCHEUER. You have got the toe in, and that is a start.

Mr. WRIGHT. It is not just happening in Detroit, and these people didn't hear about your meeting in February and come and make a noise the way I did.

Mr. SCHEUER. It may be happening some other places, but we haven't heard about it happening very much.

Mr. WRIGHT. They aren't getting the kind of coverage because they are black and because the power structure media do not recognize it.

Mr. SCHEUER. We have got roughly 175 standard metropolitan areas with a population of over 100,000; now maybe two or three or four or five have done the fascinating job that you have done. Now one of the things that this commission would do would be to give you a forum for expressing your views, and I would hope you would be in on the decisionmaking process. If such a commission were established and if this bill passes, I would use every ounce of energy and influence I had to make sure that you were a member of this commission.

Your basic concern with Negroes doing it is right. It's the philosophy that Gus Hawkins and Bill Hathaway and I helped to write in. It's quite obvious that whatever can be done by Negro leadership should be done, and that is probably the best way of progress being made.

I would like to have your experience and your success to the extent that you have had success generalized. I would like to see you in a position to exercise leadership for all of the American communities to show them the way that you have arrived at this point of progress.

You haven't achieved total success, and you admit that. You have said that you haven't been given access to the full range of the broadcast media. Again, you have come a considerable portion of the way, but because of the indifference or hostility of the white power structure as you characterize it, and we couldn't disagree with that, you haven't gone the whole way.

You are talking about getting in on Station WBAI here in New York. I know WBAI very well. It's an excellent station. It probably has a higher percentage of the egghead listening audience than any other station in the country. It's a small station, and I will warn you that it doesn't serve but a fraction of one percent of the 20 to 25 million people in the metropolitan area of New York. If you want to make progress in this city, you have to break into the major broadcast media, NBC, CBS, ABC, and the rest of them.

This to me seems to be also the challenge that you face in Detroit. One of the things that such a Presidential Commission could do would be to involve not only distinguished Negro leaders like yourself, but the presidents of the great networks and the presidents of the newspapers and the magazines—to involve them into living through this problem with you, into thinking through it with you, and maybe breaking down some of the doors of indifference or prejudice that have so far thwarted you in your effort to hit the major media.

You have done an excellent job with some of the media, but you haven't hit the full range. If you get into WBAI in New York, you will find that your listenership is composed of people like us, people who don't need what you are offering, because they are aware.

Mr. WRIGHT. I am not sure. I can get WBAI, and I would rather leave here and get interviewed there than not to get interviewed at all.

Mr. SCHEUER. The main problem is to get the dissemination of the contributions Negroes have made and are making so that the average Negro in Harlem will get it when tunes in on the media; he tunes in on channel 2, 4, 5, 7, 9, and 11, and to some extent on 13. He doesn't tune in on 13 very much. The problem that we all face is how to get the work that you are doing into the general media where not only the majority of the Negro population, but the majority of the white population tunes in.

Mr. WRIGHT. WBAI belongs to a national network of stations and the interview that I made was put into the system, and I began to get letters from grassroots people throughout the country who listen to it. I could tell where the interview was being held. These were people who wrote to us and sent contributions because they liked what we were doing. It's not a total loss.

Mr. SCHEUER. Of course it's not. I think you would agree with me that if you want to go hunting, you go where the ducks are, and the real ducks are the major television networks. Those are the doors that we have to bang down because when the average Negro or the average white American tunes in on his television set, he listens to the great network stations. It's through these stations you are going to get into those living rooms, and not primarily through WBAI or their affiliates.

Mr. WRIGHT. I think you know about Morgan's law, and he was a bank robber. Someone asked him. "Why do you rob the bank?", and he said, "That is where the money is."

Mr. SCHEUER. You're darn right. The money here is in the major media, and it seems to me that this kind of a commission that could involve the top power structure of the media as well as the top power structures of educators, people such as yourself, who could be the catalytic agent that would help break down some of those barriers to getting into the major media.

Mr. WRIGHT. I would have to revise my whole attitude with the Federal Government and my relationship with it in terms of being a

Negro. There is nothing in my experience that would allow me at this moment to say that the results that would accrue from a responsive commission about which I had nothing to say——

Mr. SCHEUER. Supposing you were a member of that commission?

Mr. WRIGHT. I don't think I could accept a position on the commission. That would be the antithesis of the things that I think should be done. Aside from the things I have mentioned to you, the intangibles are the sense of pride that the people with whom I work get from doing what they are doing, you see. And to see them emerge as whole human beings because of working at this thing and getting a reorientation about themselves as people is very satisfying.

With the Federal Government, you know, deciding the issues and controlling, you must admit that whenever the Federal Government starts managing things, things are not run the way they say they should run.

Mr. SCHEUER. We do have a program now of federal assistance to arts and humanities, and there is virtually no control exercised. It operates on exactly the principle that you advocate, namely, of making funds available where there are local people who want to do a significant local job in arts and humanities.

Mr. WRIGHT. I am glad you mentioned that because we applied to that group when we got ready to make this exhibit. They turned us down cold and said we didn't need the exhibit. We didn't get a dime and they funded $55,000 worth of non-Negro communities' progress with the year's funds in 1967. We didn't get a dime and we ran our hands in our pocket and did it ourselves. That is the only way we got it.

Mr. SCHEUER. Maybe if there were a commission that were set up with the purpose of identifying especially and solely with the problem of disseminating the contributions of Negroes, that they would spend the money on the contributions of Negroes. This would be their sole function: to design a program to disseminate through our major media the contributions that Negroes have made and are making.

Mr. HATHAWAY. I think you may find some solace in reading the first line in section 3. The commission simply conducts the studies of all proposals to create a better understanding and knowledge of Negro history and the proposals would be yours. The commission really is going to do nothing more than we are doing here today, except you will have a panel of experts who are doing it and who will be doing it for a longer period of time.

Mr. WRIGHT. Meanwhile nothing in the communities is happening. Everybody is standing waiting for the commission to decide what the great power structure is going to do.

Mr. HAWKINS. You think the people in the field are waiting on us?

Mr. WRIGHT. Yes. I have asked, and when I came to Washington I thought; what could a federal commission treat objectively the life story of DuBois and Paul Robeson and now Malcolm X.

I have read reports and several people have mentioned here today the history of the Negro with respect to Dr. Charles Drew and the blood bank thing. But I have read treatises on the history of blood banking in this country in medical journals and some of them came from Institutes of Health. They did not even mention Drew.

Mr. SCHEUER. This is what the commission is designed to cure. You have to have some confidence that maybe our government can change under pressure. I have confidence that Members of Congress are educable, that we can grow and meet the challenge of the time.

You complain about the Smithsonian. Your people in Detroit aren't really going to affect very substantially the policies of the Smithsonian Institute.

Mr. WRIGHT. We are not going to waste any time either.

Mr. SCHEUER. I feel that the problems that you have cited with the Smithsonian are very real problems and are a proper area of concern.

Mr. WRIGHT. Why haven't you done something about it?

Mr. SCHEUER. We can't as Members of Congress tell them what to do. But I think this route of setting up a Presidential commission would be more effective. The commission could have a discourse with the Smithsonian on why they are overlooking the contributions that 11 percent have made to American life—and it's only this kind of top-drawer power structure apparatus that is going to affect the Smithsonian.

It seems to me that with this concern you would want this kind of a gold-plated citizens group.

Mr. WRIGHT. You know what a Southern Congressman would do? He would just cut off the funds. They wouldn't have to have a commission. If you were going to have a commission that was not favorable to the Southern wing of your party, all they have to do is just tighten up the purse strings, and it would come out the way they wanted.

Look at the rat control bill and the rent subsidies.

Mr. SCHEUER. We ultimately passed the rat control bill and the rent program. We didn't do it the first time. The Congress laughed down that bill last summer. Congress was divided by the coalition—the conservative Democats—and they laughed it down with some jokes on the floor of the House, in poor taste.

They found out that the American people didn't appreciate their humor. Rats in the urban centers were not a laughing matter, and Congress had second thoughts, and they passed the rat control bill and rent supplemental program.

I think we ought to have a little faith that Congress is capable of growing. You do have a liberal leadership in the Congress represented by men like Hathaway and Gus Hawkins. We aren't in a majority now, but we are there. We are working our will in our modest ways and this could be a program that doesn't cost a great deal of money and that the Congress could easily pass if it had broad-range support that might effect some of the things you talk about. I don't see anything inconsistent with this bill and your program.

I see this bill would fortify your program and enable the program to be duplicated in dozens of cities.

You advocate resources coming in from the outside to stimulate resources in the Negro communities. I think this is the way this commission ought to function. If men like you were on the commission, the commission might very well end up using seed money to activate Negro leadership to do the job they do. This could be the very instrument of accomplishing what you have already accomplished in many other American communities and in helping you to do a greater job in Detroit and giving you access to the power structure and the media there.

94-721 O—68——8

I honestly don't see any contradiction between our goals and yours. In fact, I see our commission as being the instrument through which you can function on a far broader scale than you are functioning now.

Mr. BURROUGHS. I am the curator of the Museum of African-American History that Dr. Wright mentioned. As a matter of fact, your commission heard of our museum 4 years ago. When that first bill was introduced, our material was requested from you to draw up in the bill. The letters came from your office. We answered them twice, sending materials and how the museum started. We never got an answer from you.

Mr. SCHEUER. I am sorry for that if my office goofed. It frequently does.

Mr. BURROUGHS. In this case we were not invited to the last meeting in Washington, and this one I heard about through Dr. Wright, whose representative came through Chicago to report on what transpired. That is the first time we heard about it in this case.

Mr. SCHEUER. We did consult with many dozens of organizations, and if we didn't hit you, I can only apologize.

Mr. WRIGHT. His was the largest and oldest of its kind in the country. I don't see how you can possibly get to a dozen and not to his.

Mr. SCHEUER. We managed, and I apologize.

Mr. BURROUGHS. I can't speak for my whole board. I can speak for myself and several other members. We have a large board that covers the whole country and even some representatives abroad. I personally have the present intentions that Dr. Wright has. Although I wouldn't say that I am completely opposed to the commission, I do think that somehow, going back to this, I think that things could be reconsidered and this is why I am not agreeing with Mr. Innis, who spoke this morning, to a large degree. Although I share somewhat his ideas, I thought that his suggestion that the President appoint a commission, but prior to this call a conference of the black leadership across the country. Black leadership across the country or in the field would appoint the representatives after consultation with the broad mass of people who are working in the field, like Dr. Wright, people in Boston, and there are many, many, many people.

I think in this way maybe something good will come out of this, although, as I said, personally I share many of the misgivings of Dr. Wright, although I am not speaking for the board as such. I am speaking for myself and speaking for several members of the board.

Thank you.

Mr. SCHEUER. I think that is a very interesting suggestion, and what I would like you gentlemen to do is to examine the bill and then come up with some suggestions of language that you would like to see included in the bill that would clarify and make clear your emphasis that the commission should find ways and means of working cooperatively with agencies in the field that are doing a job, helping them to function more effectively and working through them wherever there was an agency like Dr. Wright's in Detroit that had considerable experience and a considerable record of success.

I am only speaking for myself now, but I would firmly support language of that kind. I hope you could help us draft something that would make it clear that where there was an agency in the field, it would be the intent of Congress that the commission would find ways and means of fortifying that agency and giving them the way to work with local groups.

This is the way the poverty program is set up, and this wouldn't be anything new and different. This wouldn't be any precedent-shattering approach. This would be with the approach that Congress has taken in many other pieces of legislation, and I think it's a completely sound approach.

I think what Dr. Wright describes as his activities in Detroit is first class, and I think that is exactly what we want to encourage. I wouldn't have any hesitancy at all in seeing language in this bill that would emphasize and make it clear that it's this kind of an approach that the Congress would favor the commission's taking.

We not only can put that language in the bill, but we can put that language in the committee report that accompanies the bill. That would state very clearly and emphatically that it's the desire of the Congress that the commission devise ways and means of working cooperatively with and fortifying the efforts of groups just like yours in Chicago and Dr. Wright's in Detroit.

Again, speaking personally, I would welcome the opportunity of sitting down with either of you gentlemen, or both of you, and actually put down the language. Now I can speak for my colleagues in saying that none of us feel that we have a monopoly on virtue or that we have all-encompassing wisdom or that we feel that we have put down the last bit of prose that conceivably could be written on the subject.

We are all beginners at this, at least the three of us on this side of the table are, and we would actively welcome the guidance and counsel that you could give us and specific language that you could come up with for this bill. Yours is a philosophy that we certainly accept, and I would be astonished if my two colleagues were not sympathetic. I find absolutely nothing inconsistent between what we are trying to accomplish and already doing and this commission. I see this commission as the engine that would enable you largely to fortify and expand the work you are doing and to break down doors that prevent you from access to major media.

I want my colleagues to respond to this.

Mr. Hawkins. This is a revelation and inspiration to me to find that there are some militant forces seeking to advance the cause of Negro history and culture. I thought everybody had gone to sleep, and I am glad to know that there are some who feel that there is a peoples' revolution out there somewhere that we need to encourage. For what little has been achieved on a national scale, I didn't think that there was anything. I am very pleased to know that we do have such militant voices.

I would do everything in the world to favor this. I think that is obvious. I agree with all the remarks that you have said, even those that you disqualified me from agreeing with you.

Mr. Scheuer. I didn't want to put words in your mouth.

Mr. Wright. Thank you for listening.

Mr. Scheuer. I am very grateful for your testimony, and we hope we will have the opportunity of working closely with you.

I wish to thank all of the witnesses for their splendid testimony which I am sure will be very useful to the members of this committee in our deliberations. I also wish to thank Mrs. Diana Zentay, a Congressional Fellow from the American Political Science Association, who has worked so intelligently and devotedly in making the arrangements for this hearing and the all-day conference in Washington, which preceded it.

The meeting of the Select Subcommittee on Labor is hereby adjourned, subject to the call of the Chair.

(Whereupon, at 5:15 p.m., the subcommittee recessed, subject to the call of the Chair.)

(The following material was submitted for the record:)

STATEMENT BY MRS. JEAN BLACKWELL HUTSON, CURATOR, SCHOMBURG COLLECTION OF NEGRO LITERATURE AND HISTORY, NEW YORK PUBLIC LIBRARY

My years of experience in the Schomburg Collection have certainly provided many instances of the fact that Negro history and culture is a matter of national and international concern. Correspondence on my desk comes from all parts of the country and most especially from the West Coast, where facilities for study in this area are much more limited than in the East. In the East there exists the Schomburg Collection, New York City, the James Weldon Johnson Memorial Collection at Yale University in New Haven, Conn., the Moorland Foundation at Howard University and the Library of Congress, both in Washington, D.C., the Slaughter and the Countee Cullen Memorial Collections at Atlanta University in Atlanta, Georgia, and the Special Collections at Fisk University in Nashville, Tennessee. The Special Collections at Fisk include the W. E. B. DuBois collection, the Edwin R. Embree Collection, the American Missionary Association archives, the Charles S. Johnson Collection, The John M. Langston Collection, The James C. Napier Collection and the Robert E. Park Collection.

Since the Schomburg Collection is the only one in a public library system, and has more museum materials than the university collections, it probably comes closer to being a model center of Negro history and culture than the others. At present, the Schomburg Collection is the nearest to a center of Negro history and culture to be found in the northeastern region, and many scholars believe it to be the greatest in existence anywhere. However, the Schomburg Collection has been the prophet who has been without honor in his homeland. Those who revere it most live far away from it, and are dazzled on infrequent visits. Mainly they are dazzled by rare books, manuscripts and art objects, collected by Arthur Schomburg before the more recent and current increase in interest in materials about Negro history and culture began.

Schomburg aspired to collect all books by authors of African descent and any books about peoples of African descent regardless of the language or of the subject content. Prints, photographs, art objects, phonographs and sheet music supplement the book collection in the attempt to record the entire experience of the Black man in world history. Because Schomburg was Puerto Rican of African ancestry and was trilingual, speaking Spanish, English and French with great facility, and because he had roamed the bookmarts of Latin America, North Africa, Spain, France and England, his collection was more international in scope than other collections of his time. It has been especially useful since the recent identification of American Negroes with contemporary black Africans and with mutual African forbears and heritage.

Mr. Schomburg used to have to beg for funds during his career as Curator of the Collection, and each of his successors have had to develop his own style of appeal for funds. Negro history materials have always been more expensive than other publications because they have been published in small quantities for a very select public. Books in this field go out of print very quickly and are then offered by dealers at rates for rare books or scarce books, which indeed they are. Thus collections in this field are more expensive than average library collections. There is also a high rate of pilferage, since the supreme compliment the American library-user pays a book is to steal it. (I refer to the case of the

Bible being stolen more than any other book.) One great strength in acquisitions for the Collection has been the sentimental attachment of the people who have been inspired by it. Many great authors of present and past have been honored to donate copies of their publications. Rulers of the newly independent nations of Africa and the Caribbean also are pleased to give newspapers and other publications reflecting recent stages of their development and reflections on long forgotten eras of their history. One way or another the book-stock of the Schomburg Collection has doubled during my years here.

It has been difficult to get qualified staff for the Schomburg Collection because the wage rates do not reward specialization. No sooner does a staff member become conversant in the field, than he is offered a better paying position in private industry or in the university field. Few people are dedicated enough to continue to perform tasks they enjoy without compensation commensurate with their ability, as have two of Schomburg's staff who have been with the collection even longer than I have.

There have been several conferences pertaining to the question if materials about Negro history and culture. I suggest that the findings of these conferences be the foundations upon which the proposed Commission should proceed: The first was a conference of librarians and historians, held at Atlanta University, October, 1965. Proceedings of this conference were published and I believe some leg-work was done following that gathering.

The Association for the Study of Negro Life and History, in at least two annual conferences, has devoted much time to discussion of the location and preservation of materials about Negro history. The Association has an ongoing project of locating manuscripts in this field.

The United Federation of Teachers sponsored a national conference on teaching Negro history which emphasized existing materials as well as the need for more materials to be used by schools.

The African Studies Association, through its Bulletin, publishes papers on existing facilities for studying African and Afro-American history in the United States.

If the Commission can work on the basis of these established findings, its work may proceed quickly and efficiently. Perhaps it can report in less than the estimated year's time.

Testimony of National Urban League

The National Urban League is a professional community service organization founded in 1910 to secure equal opportunity for Negro citizens and other minorities. It is tax exempt, non-partisan and interracial in its leadership and staff.

The National Urban League has affiliates in eighty-seven (87) cities and thirty-three (33) states and in the District of Columbia. It maintains national headquarters in New York City.

A trained professional staff conducts the day-to-day activities of the Urban League, using the techniques and disciplines of social work in performing its services. This staff throughout the country numbers more than 800 paid employees whose operations are re-inforced by 8,000 volunteers who bring expert knowledge and experience to racial matters.

We appreciate this invitation to appear before your Committee to add to your body of knowledge the information and evidence that we have accumulated over the years as experts in the area and subject which are now before this Committee.

The National Urban League would be woefully remiss in discharging its obligation to the Negro minority of 18,871,000 and to the total United States population of 179,320,000 descendants of migrants, if our organization did not at this time, endorse the concept of H.R. 12962, providing for the establishment of a Commission on Negro History and Culture. We view the bill as an educational measure, offering a positive challenge to resisters to change.

The accomplishment of this goal must not be prolonged. Early Urban League efforts to "get a message" to the nation on this subject are now history. In 1926, the then Urban League Executive Director, Eugene Kinkle Jones, supported by our National Board, prevailed upon the Carnegie Corporation to present as a gift, the Schomburg Collection of 4,000 volumes and over 1,200 pamphlets and prints to the New York Public Library. For over four decades remaining as the largest African and American Negro History Collection in the world, continuing and unspeakable neglect of the Collection is now also history.

The beginnings of Negro history on the North American Continent go back to its discovery and exploration. The beginnings of Negro history in New York City were established with holes dug for trading posts and fortifications built against the Indian landholders. Years later, segregated Negro burial grounds were excavated and carted away to make way for subways to better transport new immigrants to upper parts of Manhattan, where he, the Negro, had first built the roads. So the story can be duplicated in villages, towns and major cities from Main to Texas and New York to California.

The story of the Negroes' contribution to United States and world culture must not only be preserved and disseminated; its fragmented, decaying and lost records must be unearthed and restored in order to re-establish the pride of those whose forebears helped to build the Nation's economy.

The establishment of the Commission now under consideration followed by rapid execution of its recommendations, would lessen the feeling of neglect on the part of many and feelings of bitterness on the part of others who know that thirteen Presidents of the United States since the emancipation of slaves, listened to the cries of Negroes, but would not hear them.

Such a Commission could become a reference point for those doing research on all levels of interest. Offering official status and recognition of this area of study will make a legitimate area of knowledge for all Americans. Hopefully, execution of the Commission's recommendations will influence school curricula throughout the country. By no small consideration, execution of the Commission's recommendations will enable the American Negro to more fully enter the mainstream of American life. The urgent need to close these gaps cannot be over-emphasized.

We wish to enthusiastically congratulate the architests of Bill H.R. 12962 and simultaneously state areas where we are not in full agreement with the planers or where we feel obvious omissions in the Bill should be included at this time.

1. Based on the fact that we have reached a lost frontier in race relations in the United States, with no pot holes for those who retreat, it would seem that an allowance of *at least twelve months after the enactment of the act* is too long for the report to reach the President.

2. It would perhaps be advantageous to include in the findings of the report, the suggestion that *all government-aided libraries would be requested* or *invited* to fully utilize all materials disseminated through channels approved or recommended by the Commission.

Having noted these areas of disagreement, may we again state our enthusiastic endorsement of the Bill.

U.S. SENATE,
Washington, D.C., April 3, 1968.

Hon. JAMES H. SCHEUER,
Longworth House Office Building,
Washington, D.C.

DEAR CONGRESSMAN SCHEUER: I commend and applaud the efforts of the House and Senate sponsors of this measure and extend my warm thanks to those who have organized to support it.

As you very aptly observed, one of the often overlooked consequences of the history of the Negro in America has been the almost total absence of any feeling for his historical and cultural heritage. It is unfortunate that American society as a whole has little knowledge of the quality and extent of the cultural background of so significant a segment of this nation's population. But it is a tragic fact that in far too many cases Negro citizens themselves demonstrate so little interest in their own historical antecedents and cultural worth.

It is clear, of course, that recognition of the American Negro's cultural heritage can be no substitute for the present recognition of individual and group worth which is the promise of the United States Constitution. But I think it can fairly be said that the two are integrally related. If America as a whole accepts the Negro as an individual with a proud culture and a significant history, then surely we will have taken a conspicuous step toward realization of the guarantee of real equality.

I believe that the bill you introduced, H.R. 12962, to which S.2979 is the companion bill, is legislation of significance. I am proud to be associated with it. I hope the both houses of Congress will act promptly and favorably upon it. I am sure that with the devoted help of the Committee being formed by Mr. Wilkins, Mr. Young, and Mr. Wesley, the chances for success have been greatly enhanced.

It goes without saying that you can count on my fullest and most enthusiastic cooperation.

Sincerely yours,

EDWARD W. BROOKE,
U.S. Senator from Massachusetts.

STATEMENT OF HON. DON EDWARDS, A REPRESENTATIVE IN CONGRESS FROM THE STATE OF CALIFORNIA

What do we know about the Negro's history in the United States? What do we know about the brutality he has suffered and the humiliation he has endured? What do we know about his dreams, and the dreams of his ancestors; his accomplishments, and those of his ancestors?

As the recent panel dicussion on the establishment of a Commission on Negro History and Culture made perfectly clear, we know all too little. And what we do know often bears no relationship to reality. At that discussion in Washington last month, I was particularly struck by the characterization of slavery in the textbooks our children are reading today as 'humane and necessary'.

This distortion of the role of the Negro in the cultural mosiac that is America today is more than just a problem for scholars. Ignorance about the contributions to American history and culture by the Negro is a sword with a sharp double edge—one that re-enforces fear and prejudice among the whites, the other that cuts deep into the self esteem of the blacks.

The National Advisory Commission on Civil Disorders recently shook the roots of complacency by reporting that "Our nation is moving toward two societies, one black, one white—separate and unequal." The sword of ignorance continues to widen this chasm. If we can devote some effort to recording the history and cultural contribution of the Negro, before the facts and artifacts become impossible to decipher, this would be a giant step in the direction of reconciliation. Indeed, this is a critical area for action to be added to the important suggestions presented in the Commission's Report.

It will undoubtedly be a difficult task, for it is necessary to first undo the damage of centuries of neglect. Historical documents and material now dispersed throughout the country, and perhaps throughout the world, must be brought together. There is a rich and extensive history to uncover, that originates with the very birth of our nation, and contributes throughout to its growth.

But the longer we accept the "do-nothing" attitude of the past, the more history will be lost to the future. There is a great deal of work to be done, and we must get moving. We must break that double-edged sword, before we let it further divide our society in two.

TESTIMONY BY HON. JOSEPH Y. RESNICK, A REPRESENTATIVE IN CONGRESS FROM THE STATE OF NEW YORK

Mr. Chairman, thank you for the opportunity to testify on H.R. 12962.

The American Negro has been short-changed in this country in far too many ways. In general, he is ill-fed, ill-clothed, ill-housed, and ill-educated. He is at the same time both blamed for his plight and pushed further into it by white Americans.

The recent report of the President's Riot Commission tells, perhaps not even strongly enough, just what is happening in this country and what will continue to happen unless we act immediately.

We have taken steps to initiate programs which will begin to alleviate some of the problems, but there is much to be done.

The report pointed out that in addition to being deprived materially, the Negro has been and is being deprived culturally and historically, as well. Perhaps this is not as gnawing a deprivation as the absence of sufficient food, clothing, or shelter, but it is as unjust a deprivation, nonetheless.

The background of the American Negro is rich in a history and tradition that is largely unknown and unrecognized by most Negroes, as well as whites. His culture spans two continents and many more centuries than does the history of white mankind. His history is novel in that it is unlike that of the Anglo-Saxon. And yet, his achievements have been overlooked, or at best, slightly mentioned in American history books.

While there have been attempts made to document Afro-American history, and to commorate the achievements of Negroes through the centuries, these attempts have been feeble, due to the lack of funds and facilities.

H.R. 12962 would take the first important step toward rightful recognition of the American Negro's place in American history. This bill, which I and 15 of my colleagues have co-sponsored, would create a Presidential Commission on Negro History and Culture.

The Commission would be composed of 11 members who are recognized authorities on Negro history and culture, and whose job it would be to report to the President, after one year's work, on all aspects of the collection, preservation and ultimate integration of events in Negro history into the mainstream of American history.

Mr. Chairman, it has been said that he who has nothing to look backward to with pride has nothing to look forward to with hope. I strongly urge this subcommittee to report favorably on H.R. 12962 so that all Americans can look backward with pride on the history of our Afro-Americans and look forward with hope to a just America for all her citizens.

STATEMENT BY HON. CLARENCE J. BROWN, JR., A REPRESENTATIVE IN CONGRESS FROM THE STATE OF OHIO

On Monday, April 8th, I plan to introduce a bill to establish a National Museum and Repository of Negro History and Culture at Wilberforce, Ohio. Eleven of my colleagues from both sides of the aisle (see note, below) have stated that they wish to join in sponsoring this legislation since they share my belief that there is a particular need at this point in our Nation's history for such a museum.

The museum, when established, will contain evidence of Negro contributions to arts and letters, science and technology, religion, politics, education and entertainment, as well as other areas. The museum will also serve as a center for research in Negro history and culture.

The Wilberforce area was a center of the abolition movement and the main line of the Underground Railroad operated to assist slaves fleeing to the North during the mid-1800's.

Two predominantly Negro universities, Wilberforce University and Central State University, are located in Wilberforce. Wilberforce University, founded in 1856, was the first Negro institution of higher learning in the United States; Central State University was founded in 1887. Officials from both universities have urged the creation of the proposed museum.

My bill authorizes the Secretary of the Interior to establish the museum and to acquire the required land and buildings through funds to be made available by the federal government, as well as from gifts and donations. The Secretary is authorized to consult and cooperate with the officials of Wilberforce and with appropriate historical societies and other interested persons concerning the development and operation of this museum.

I feel that the unfortunate events which occurred during the week following the assassination of Dr. Martin Luther King attest to the idea that our Nation needs the reconciliation between the races which can be fostered by the museum I have proposed. Certainly, our unique American culture is a living, vital thing which changes with every passing year. Many racial and ethnic backgrounds have contributed to that culture. Among these contributions, the Negro ranks high in what he has given to our society in the fields I have mentioned. There should be a place where all Americans can go and see graphically demonstrated the nature of these contributions. There should be a place where Negro Americans can share the pride of their participation in American life.

(NOTE.—H.R. 16507, to which Congressman Brown refers in his letter, was introduced in the House on April 8, under the sponsorship of Mr. Brown of Ohio, Mr. Anderson of Illinois, Mr. Ashley, Mr. Feighan, Mr. Lukens, Mr. Miller of

Ohio, Mr. Mosher, Mr. Taft, Mr. Tiernan, Mr. Vanik and Mr. Whelan. The text is printed below.)

[H.R. 16507, 90th Cong., second sess.]

A BILL To authorize the Secretary of the Interior to establish and operate a National Museum and Repository of Negro History and Culture at or near Wilberforce, Ohio

Be it enacted by the Senate and House of Representatives of the United States of America in Congress assembled, That the Secretary of the Interior (hereafter referred to as the "Secretary") shall establish a museum which shall be known as the National Museum and Repository of Negro History and Culture in which shall be preserved, collected, and displayed, for the advancement of public interest and knowledge, objects, relics, and records pertaining to Negro participation in, and contributions to, the history and culture of the United States. The Secretary is authorized and directed—

(1) to acquire by gift, purchase with appropriations or donated funds, transfer from any Federal agency, exchange, or otherwise, suitable land (together with any buildings or other improvements thereon) and interests in land in the vicinity of Wilberforce, Ohio, for the location of such museum,

(2) to maintain and operate such museum, either in an existing structure acquired under provisions of paragraph (1) or in a building or buildings constructed by him for such purpose, and

(3) to construct access roads, parking areas, and other appropriate facilities for museum visitors.

SEC. 2. (a) The Secretary is authorized to cooperate with Central State University and Wilberforce University and with historical societies and other interested persons in the maintenance and operation of the museum and may seek the assistance of and consult with such universities, societies, and persons from time to time with respect to matters concerning the development and operation of the museum.

(b) The Secretary may accept on behalf of the people of the United States gifts of historic objects, relics, and records pertaining to Negro history and culture for appropriate display or other use in keeping with the purposes for which such museum is established.

SEC. 3. There are hereby authorized to be appropriated such sums of money as may be necessary to carry out the purposes of this Act.

THE ATLANTA CONSTITUTION,
Atlanta, Ga., March 7, 1968.

Hon. JAMES H. SCHEUER,
U.S. House of Representatives,
Washington, D.C.

DEAR CONGRESSMAN SCHEUER: I salute you for having introduced H.R. 12962, which would create a Presidentially appointed Commission on Negro History and Culture that would consider all aspects of this area of neglect.

I cannot be present for the sub-committee hearing, but out of a life-long experience in the South, I am convinced that the submergence of the Negro's culture and historical contributions to this country has been, and is, one of the root causes of the disenchantment of the educated Negro with our present society. The elimination of the Negro's contribution has been a deliberate thing. It was part and parcel of many other factors which prevented the Negro from having pride in being a Negro and in being American. There is a very considerable body of historical and cultural contribution. I think we would do a national service if this could be brought forthrightly to the attention of all the people and if we could move to have it made a proper part of all books and literature dealing with the subject.

Sincerely yours,

RALPH MCGILL, *Publisher.*

STATEMENT BY AMERICAN ASSOCIATION OF MUSEUMS

The American Association of Museums, representating museums of history, science, and art, as well as many museum professionals and interested individuals, supports the purposes of H.R. 12962.

The collection, preservation, and interpretation of historical objects of American culture is of major interest to the Association and to all American museums. One of the chief purposes of a museum is to use the cultural evidence of the past for the enlightenment and education of the present generation, while conserving this heritage and adding new evidence for future generations.

Although the provision of financial aid to any museum lies outside the scope of the Association's activities, if the proposed Museum of Negro History and Culture is established, it can count on the advice and assistance which the Association provides to all its institutional members.

AMERICAN SOCIOLOGICAL ASSOCIATION,
Washington, D.C., March 4, 1968.

Hon. JAMES H. SCHEUER,
U.S. House of Representatives,
Washington, D.C.

DEAR MR. SCHEUER: Thank you for your letter of February 28, and the enclosed copy of H.R. 12962, a Bill to provide for the establishment of a Commission on Negro History and Culture. In responding I wish to make it clear, first of all, that my comments on this Bill are entirely personal, reflecting my nearly 25 years in professional sociology, and in no way are to be interpreted as representing a position of the American Sociological Association, of which I am Executive Officer.

The Bill you propose is, in my judgment, not only exciting but long overdue. From my own professional reading in sociology and anthropology I am aware of certain aspects of Negro history and culture, and of the many contributions of Negroes of various nations to the mainstreams of civilization. Yet I fully recognize also that my knowledge is limited and superficial—and I would assume that the same can be said for most people. The systematic collection and preservation of relevant data would mark a giant step forward in an unusually important and interesting area, and I sincerely hope that your Bill will receive prompt consideration and passage.

There are several specific points to be emphasized:

1. The proposed Commission is expected to submit its report "not later than twelve months after the date of enactment of this Act." This, it seems to me, is much too short a time for such an important undertaking. Time will elapse between the date of enactment and the appointment of the Commission. The Commission itself must get organized; staff members must be obtained; other logistical problems will be encountered—all of which diminish the actual time that will be devoted to the important tasks at hand. Given these considerations, I would strongly urge that the life of the Commission be extended to at least two years from the date of enactment, so that thorough and proper consideration can be given to the significant problems involved.

2. The Commission itself must be chosen with great care. The proposed Bill mentions "persons who are authorities on Negro history and culture," and this is an absolute necessity if the great purposes of the Commission are to be attained. But I have a strong impression that appointments to many Commissions are based on considerations other than expertise or knowledge, that many persons so appointed simply represent different political "fronts." It would be most unfortunate should this happen to the proposed Commission. I would hope that you and your colleagues supporting the Bill will be in a position to canvass various professional disciplines—history, anthropology, archaeology, sociology, language, music, etc.—so that the best possible professionals can be recruited to the very demanding tasks that will be presented. Law and religion are other fields that should be represented. I think the success of the entire enterprise depends upon the calibre, understanding, and dedication of the persons appointed to the Commission, and this sentiment should accompany transmission of the Bill from Congress to the White House.

In sum, it should be apparent that the proposed Bill has my hearty personal endorsement, and if there is any further way that I can be of assistance, before or after passage, please let me know.

With all best wishes,

Sincerely,

E. H. VOLKART, *Executive Officer.*

SOUTHERN REGIONAL COUNCIL, INC.,
Atlanta, Ga., March 5, 1968.

Hon. JAMES H. SCHEUER,
House of Representatives,
Congress of the United States,
Washington, D.C.

MY DEAR CONGRESSMAN SCHEUER: You are to be commended on your efforts to create a Commission on Negro History and Culture.

I am in complete agreement with the need for such a commission and feel a sense of urgency about it. There is a great amount of culture and history that is important to the nation and the longer we wait the more difficult it will be to remedy this situation. Indeed, unless we act soon much of this rich heritage which has done so much to shape all of us will be lost forever.

Sincerely yours,

PAUL ANTHONY, *Executive Director.*

GREENBURGH SCHOOL DISTRICT NO. 8,
Hartsdale, N.Y., March 18, 1968.

Hon. JAMES H. SCHEUER,
Bronx, N.Y.

DEAR CONGRESSMAN SCHEUER: I am most pleased to see that H.R. 12962 has been proposed as a bill to submit to Congress. You are probably aware that Greenburgh School District No. 8 of Hartsdale, New York has been an integrated school district since 1951 and has been a leader in intercultural education.

Under our own impetus we have been attempting to establish, on a small scale, the same type of reference center that your bill proposed. I wish to go on record for our school district as being in full support of the objectives this legislation is proposing to achieve.

If there is any way that we can provide support for your proposal, feel free to call upon us.

Sincerely yours,

IRVING MILLER, *Administrative Assistant.*

THE AFRICAN METHODIST EPISCOPAL CHURCH,
COMMISSION OF SOCIAL ACTION,
Sumter, S.C., March 5, 1968.

Hon. JAMES H. SCHEUER,
House of Representatives,
Washington, D.C.

DEAR SIR: The African Methodist Episcopal Church Commission on Social Action extends its profoundest salute to you and to your Congressional Committee upon the introduction of H.R. Bill 12962.

The establishment of such a Commission on Negro History and Culture is long overdue from both the standpoint of national sociological propriety and also that of racial cultural appreciation.

We shall follow with eager expectation your progress.

Sincerely,

F. C. JAMES, *Consultant.*

THE ASSOCIATION FOR THE STUDY OF NEGRO LIFE AND HISTORY,
NEW YORK BRANCH, INC.,
St. Albans, N.Y., March 22, 1968.

Hon. JAMES H. SCHEUER,
Congress of the United States,
House of Representatives,
Washington, D.C.

DEAR CONGRESSMAN SCHEUER: I wish to express my sincere thanks for your letter of March 11, inviting me to attend the hearings to create a Presidentially appointed Commission on Negro History and Culture. You were very careful to inidcate the room, floor, address and time; however, you failed to indicate the date. Please don't feel embarrassed, as I have been guilty of this oversight myself.

I read the account in the New York Times and I am certain that it was a most successful and informative meeting. I would indeed appreciate a copy of the hearings.

I am not one of advocate Negro history for the sake of singling out Negro history. But scholar and layman alike must admit that the presence of the Negro people in America has had such a tremendous influence on historical developments and is continuing to have influence on America's historical development.

It is impossible to drain the Negro influence on American history and still have an American history.

On the psychological and sociological aspect, the dearth and distorted emphasis on the cultural and historical contributions of the Negro in America has had an unwholesome impact on the Negro's self image. The results have been obvious—millions upon millions of dollars in destruction obvious.

I believe that the most important emergency which demands a serious investigation into the promulgation of Negro history is the fact that all of the militant organizations and champions use Negro history as their main propaganda material. They proceed to teach our youth what we have failed to teach them ourselves; and of course our youth follow and believe those who have opened their eyes to what is so carefully labeled as "the truth".

We thank you for your interest, and if I can be of future assistance, please don't hesitate to contact me.

I cannot overemphasize the importance of Executive and Legislative interest in this field.

Sincerely,

ARCHIE J. PALMER, *President.*

AFRO-AMERICAN NEWSPAPERS,
Baltimore, Md., March 12, 1968.

Hon. JAMES H. SCHEUER,
House of Representatives,
Washington, D.C.

DEAR SIR: This comes to congratulate you for introducing H.R. 12962 which would create a Presidentially-appointed Commission on Negro History and Culture.

This seems to be a good bill, a meaningful first step in a program which would correct past distortions and point up achievements of colored Americans.

The idea of a commission, which I presume would be composed of historians and thoughtful literary people, would go a long way in filling a void of too-long duration.

There is a great need for preserving and collecting historical materials about Negro history and culture. We here at the AFRO are happy to add our endorsement to your very thoughtful legislation.

Very truly yours,

JOHN H. MURPHY III, *President.*

STATEMENT OF DR. ROBERT L. ZANGRANDO, ASSISTANT EXECUTIVE SECRETARY, AMERICAN HISTORICAL ASSOCIATION

Mr. Chairman and Members of the Select Subcommittee on Labor of the House Committee on Education and Labor: I appreciate this opportunity to offer testimony on the behalf of the Bill, H.R. 12962, "A Bill to Provide for the Establishment of a Commission on Negro History and Culture." I should make it clear from the beginning that I am not testifying officially in my capacity as an Officer of the American Historical Association, nor do my remarks represent any official position of the Association. However, I think it true that my role as an Officer of the largest professional historical association in the country, and my own interest and involvement in the history of minority groups in the United States (as a field for my own professional research and writing) offer me two important vantage points from which to judge the merits of this proposed legislation. I wish to speak in favor of the bill.

During the past quarter-century, this nation has been increasingly concerned with the question of race relations. A complex sequence of diverse events, both domestic and international, has forced the American people, black and white, to attend to this question in a fashion and to a degree quite unprecedented in the nation's experience. We have found ourselves repeatedly grasping for an understanding of the present in terms of the forces and factors that helped shape the history of race relations in this country, and in terms of our hopes for formulating policy in a positive, remedial, and corrective way for the future. Central to this process of assessing the past and judging the future, if either is to be done with any success, is the process of self-awareness that is so inextricably linked with historical knowledge. This proposed legislation, H.R. 12962, then, takes on a special degree of importance because of the vital contributions it can make to the development of a healthy and effective national self-awareness on the matter of interracial relations. Since rational action is tied to perception and understanding, we need to develop varied instruments for assessing the past and augmenting our understanding of the role of the Negro in America. This is of crucial importance to black and white alike, and it is on this ground that the bill merits recommendation.

Americans desperately need to understand the nature of race relations in this country. They must comprehend the extent of racial injustice and the historical elements that contributed to that injustice. At the same time, it is essential that they develop an awareness of the important contributions which the Negro has made to the American experience, and they must sense the strength and weaknesses that have characterized the efforts toward interracial reform in the past, so that they will be able in more efficient and meaningful terms to identify and implement steps for remedial action in the months and years ahead. On these grounds, the proposed legislation merits support.

The recently released Report of the National Advisory Commission on Civil Disorders indicates that we have become a very divided nation. The likelihood and hazard of further divisive conditions seem enormous. And yet, we cannot allow ourselves to be intimidated by the enormity of the problem; the proposed legislation offers a very effective and meaningful step for corrective action. Certainly this bill alone will not prove singularly sufficient to meet the crisis of race relations in this country, but it would represent an important element in the total mosaic that we must fashion to improve relations among black and white Americans. The idea of a Presidentially-appointed Commission to study all proposals leading to the creation of a better understanding of Negro history and culture, and to make recommendations to the President and to the Congress with regard to effective legislative enactments to implement such proposals, has intrinsic merit and should not be viewed simply as a hastily-fashioned response to crisis. The fact that the proposed legislation would help to meet a pressing public need for knowledge is simply a further compelling reason for approving of an idea that possesses basic substantive merit regardless of the external pressures of contemporary events.

Americans have not done a very good job of explaining themselves to each other. In no phase of our national experience is this more strikingly true than in the case of the role and contributions of the Negro in the American past. Black and white Americans alike urgently need to be educated and re-educated on these matters, and the proposed legislation. H.R. 12962, represents a very logical step toward that necessary education. Only on the basis of such a healthy and heightened awareness of the contributions that Negroes have made to our history and culture, can white and Negro Americans alike discard many of the negative, dysfunctional, and false stereotypes that have impeded effective race relations.

This proposed legislation has much to recommend it. To begin with, it looks to a deliberate examination of the historical and cultural contributions of the American Negro. Such an assessment would draw heavily upon history as a discipline, but it would also encourage the utilization of knowledge and methodological approaches from the other fields of learning in humanities and in the social studies. Such a multidisciplinary approach to the question of Negro history and culture must be applauded and encouraged on the grounds that it will significantly enrich our understanding of the Negro and of American race relations. If I may say, it is precisely for this very reason that this year's annual meeting of the Organization of American Historians (scheduled to take place in Dallas, Texas, April 18–20) will have as one of its sessions the examination of "Teaching the History of the Negro American: A Multidisciplinary Approach." Similarly, I can say that the April, 1968 issue of the *AHA Newsletter* will contain the brief but vital essay by Professor August Meier, entitled "Black America as a Research Field: Some Comments," which suggests certain areas of historical investigation in Negro history that need and would profit from the multidisciplinary approach. The proposed Presidentially-appointed Commission would represent a splendid vehicle by which to coordinate the current and planned interests and activities represented by research scholars in history and in other areas of the humanities and the social sciences, by museum curators and archivists, by teachers and students of Negro history. Such a Commission could focus attention upon and serve as a clearing house for information, suggestions, and recommendations about the study and assessment of Negro history and culture and about the most effective ways of disseminating knowledge in these areas to the public at large. As indicated in Section 3 of H.R. 12962, one of the most crucial responsibilities which such a Commission would have stems from the task of developing and suggesting ways in which valid historical information on the Negro can best be disseminated and integrated into the main stream of American education, life, and, eventually, what we rather loosely refer to as "common knowledge."

A Presidentially-appointed Commission on the order proposed in the bill would have a unique opportunity, at an important and crucial period in our national experience, to gauge our present knowledge of Negro history, to determine what gaps and deficiencies exist in our knowlegde of Negro history and culture, to focus upon ongoing efforts to augment our knowledge, and to help fashion effective programs for the future enrichment of our knowledge in these important areas. The work of such a Commission would hold vast implications for the work of scholars, teachers, students, curators, archivists, and the public at large. It is an opportunity which we must not let escape us. Conceivably the investigations and findings of the Commission could strikingly affect the teaching of Negro history and culture in schools and colleges of the country; they could markedly alter the course and emphases of graduate training programs in history and related areas; they could intensify the professional training programs of curators and archivists; they could highlight the uses to which modern, computerized technology might be put in assembling, cataloguing, and retrieving data on Negro history and culture for use in both teaching and research; they could enlarge the opportunities and scope of historical research on the Negro in America; and they could significantly expand the mental horizons of our citizens—white and Negro alike—on the important question of Negro history and culture. All of these things need to be done. There is no necessary order of priority, nor is there any one or a combination of these items that we can conveniently, and without hazard, dismiss from consideration; they all form part of a mosaic and of a network central to the development of an effective national awareness of the role and contributions of the Negro in American life.

The proposed Commission and the very promising functions it could perform readily merit endorsement by scholars because of their professional commitment to knowledge on the one hand and because of their concern as citizens on the other. I am happy to go on record as having formally endorsed H.R. 12962 on both grounds.

Howard N. Meyer

Overcoming the White Man's History

REPRINTED FROM
THE MASSACHUSETTS REVIEW
AMHERST, MASS. 01002

VOL. VII NO. 3
1966

OBSERVER

OVERCOMING THE WHITE MAN'S HISTORY

Howard N. Meyer

EVERY PHASE of the movement for equal rights has produced results that have been of benefit to *all* Americans, white and non-white. The struggle to defend freedom of speech and press for abolitionists not only won converts to their cause but aided all dissenters. The neglected education of the children of the poor whites was ended by the fine work of the biracial Reconstruction legislatures. The process of restoring the Fourteenth Amendment to the dimensions originally envisaged by its framers (a process that has been unfairly called "expansion" even by liberals who should know better) is one that helps to protect white as well as black against all forms of legal lynching. The battle of Selma has contributed not only to the fight for voting rights, but also to advance the cause of protection for all peaceful protest, on any subject, by any group.

There has been a thaw of late in one seemingly less dramatic area that has a far wider potential than its significance to the Negro alone. Until recent years the mainstream of American history has appeared to have a frozen white surface. There was a kind of shadow history underneath, a truth that all Negro scholars knew and that the uneducated sensed. All but a tiny handful of whites knew nothing about their real heritage. After the ice was broken in the fight for justice to the Negro, there began to surface other important and neglected aspects of the indigenous American radical tradition.

The whole truth about the whole of our past is needed as much outside the schools as within. The impotence of a minority to achieve social justice, even when aroused and militant, has recently prompted talk of "neo-Populism." Yet, one cannot adapt the idea of Populism to the needs of the present without a fuller understanding of the faults as well as the virtues of the mass insurgency of the '90s. The gains made by the partisans of the "Negro History" movement open the door to a new hearing for the forgotten rebel voices of the American past. "You realize," as James Baldwin said, "that if *you* are not in the history books, a great many other things must be left out of the history books too."

This was a figure of speech, as Baldwin would be the first to admit; for the grievance has not been merely, or even primarily, the simple *absence* of the Negro from the pages of history. It is a measure of the intimacy of the connection of our educational systems with the forces making for rationalization and perpetuation of racism that primers, science books, and histories long excluded dark faces from the very illustrations. When civil rights became *chic*, it was seriously suggested by one convert that sticker-pictures be provided for insertion, as if this would make things right until the next printing. With respect to American history the evils that have to be remedied go far beyond the addition of pictures and achievements. It is important that students and the adult mis-educated learn more, much more, than the catalog of omitted items: such as that Elijah McCoy, whose 1872 invention of an advanced lubricating-system fathered the phrase "it's the real McCoy," was the son of fugitive slaves, or that the valor of a black regiment saved Teddy Roosevelt and his Rough Riders from ignominious defeat at San Juan Hill. The omission of such items is more instructive than their content.

The breadth and depth of the idea of "Negro History," as agitated for half a century by a Negro-led organization that never made a front page headline in the white press, is a challenge to the foundation and structure of an entire academic discipline. The Establishment has now blandly but only nominally accepted it. It hopes, perhaps, to contain it and to restrict it to the notion of finding a "place" for the "contribution" of this "minority" to the American heritage. There are other important facets to the Negro History idea that must be integrated within the framework of American History—enough to require a complete overhaul.

1965 was the Golden Anniversary year of the Association for the Study of Negro Life and History, an organization concerning which, I suspect, most white liberals and radicals know very little. Those who have encountered the name of the organization are likely to have pigeon-holed and dismissed it as a purely intra-racial and rather exotic sort of affair, of no more concern to them than is the African Methodist Episcopal Church. One wonders how many university libraries (let alone those of secondary schools) subscribe to its principal publication, the *Journal of Negro History;* one suspects that, at least until relatively recently, even holders of the Ph.D. in history ignored it or failed fully to utilize it. It is also to the point to suggest that

94-721 O - 68 - 9

few of the popular writers, award-winning or otherwise, of the recent cascade of books on "the problem" had consulted its pages.

The *Journal* is a quarterly publication, produced on a low budget. It has appeared regularly for five decades and its bound volumes, by now, constitute a storehouse crammed with the contributions of Negro and white scholars. There are several broad headings under which this work can be grouped, long neglected in past United States historical writing and still omitted in text writing and most popularizations. These categories would include:

(a) the extent to which the "American heritage" consists of the oppression of the Negro—a picture that must be drawn in all its grim details to understand the residual effects of that oppression on both Negro and white;

(b) the scope and character of the resistance to that oppression, both within and without the ranks of its victims; and especially the advantages to all Americans of the struggle for the equality of the Negro;

(c) the degree to which the work of the white historian of the past —in some cases of the present—has itself been a tool of oppression. (One may include in this category some fascinating passages of legal history, such as found in an *exposé* in one *Journal* piece, of the fraudulent miscitation of authorities in the prevailing opinion in *Plessy v Ferguson.*);

(d) the fact, in all of its ramifications, that Africa is our mother country as much as England and Europe; that there is blended in our culture, in varying degrees in every branch, an African heritage that is no less significant than that of the "West"; that there is as much to be recalled with pride in the histories of the African tribes as in the European.

The Association for the Study of Negro Life and History, the *Journal* and a younger, less scholarly, *Bulletin,* as well as many other publications of the Association, were all launched by one man, Carter G. Woodson. Holder of the Ph.D. from Harvard ('12), this son of slaves had worked in coal mines in his native West Virginia as a boy and entered his first formal school at the age of twenty, before embarking on an academic career that was to win him the post of Dean in two colleges. The promise of a career of advancement within the ranks of the black bourgeoisie did not tempt him further, after he had become possessed of a sense of his mission. The year that saw the unveiling of *The Birth of a Nation* as the dramatic embodiment and permanent symbol of the sins of our historiography produced, as it were, the prescription for the antidote.

The point that Woodson perceived was that racism, as the product of an aggregate of false beliefs about a people, could be combatted best by the proof and publication of the truths that would dispel those beliefs. The dedicated energy that almost single-handedly seemed to sustain the A.S.N.L.H. during its early years was nourished by his inspired perception that he was forging an instrument of his people's fight for freedom. There are some intelligent and articulate "civil rights" leaders who do not quite understand this, and who neglect the tool he bequeathed them.

Some scholars and intellectuals, even today, will raise their eyebrows in skeptical disapproval of the suggestion that the white American historian has been a 'tool of oppression.' Most of these do understand, looking overseas, why the rewriting of history begins, as an implement of thought control, almost immediately after the broadcasting stations have been taken over and the Secret Police reorganized following a power shift. They cannot bring themselves to believe, however, that their own colleagues and predecessors at home have been employed in an indigenous American "Ministry of Truth." Erich Fromm, for one, in discussing Orwell's *1984*, correctly insists that those who see in its treatment of the abuses of history "only another denunciation of Stalinism" were missing the point. The process, Fromm suggests, of distorting the past in an effort to control the future is one that has been taking place continuously in the West. Somehow those who have welcomed a Fulbright's exposure of the self-created myths that imprison popular thinking about foreign affairs are not ready to confront the origin of the stereotypes that inhibit genuine unity among the masses of the poor and that impede an alliance between the poor and lower middle class.

As more and more legislation is enacted with the stated purpose of eliminating discrimination in the way people treat each other, little is done to change the way people think about each other. The moral dividends of direct non-violent action are not at all to be underestimated; one may still validly insist that effects be tackled with some understanding of their causes. Roy Wilkins once pointed out that the caricature of the Negro bequeathed us by *The Birth of a Nation* haunts many of those who react hysterically to the threat of token desegregation in the South or intrusions upon "neighborhood" school patterns in the North. Those who discuss "next steps" in the civil rights revolution are sometimes inattentive to the causes of the backward steps occurring in their presence.

The activity of the lay section of the Negro History movement—which may be described as centered within the chapters of the A.S.N.L.H., augmented by an active Chicago-based group called the Amistad Society (after a slave ship whose cargo mutinied and won) as well as a number of NAACP and CORE chapters—has consisted in transmiting the work of scholars to an agitational level. They have battled the belief in Negro inferiority that is rooted in the concept of an inferior past performance. The principal source of the documentation, by fact and analysis, that has equipped the movement to challenge school boards and text book manufacturers has been the publication of papers in the *Journal of Negro History*. These provide as well the material and much of the inspiration for the current neo-revisionist school of American historiography. What tends to distinguish historians of this new school from their predecessors and colleagues is a willingness to accept the premise that the Negro is and always has been entirely human.

Until the "new" school began to develop in the last two decades, the work that Woodson and his followers (able scholars like Charles H. Wesley, Saunders Redding, Rayford W. Logan, Lawrence D. Reddick, Benjamin Quarles, John Hope Franklin and others less well-known) did was to create a "Negro History" that was itself an involuntarily segregated product—separate from the American history of which it was entitled to be an integral part. The white school administrator and teacher, editor and publisher—all conspired to force this artificially separate development of what was obviously not a separate discipline. This co-existence of "two histories" has survived almost completely on the secondary school level, whence the dropouts and high school graduates who enter adult life, even today, with racist notions.

The injustices, the inaccuracies, the distortions, the omissions that have been the targets of the Negro History movement have by no means been confined to the period of the First Reconstruction. They are, and long have been, focussed on the 1865-77 period for functional reasons that make the analogy to Orwell painfully valid. The perfectly ghastly course that race relations took in the United States, from about 1875 onward, required nothing less than the nullification of the Fourteenth and Fifteenth Amendments. Even the Thirteenth

Amendment had been violated in spirit, for as Clarence Darrow suggested in a speech six decades ago (and the SNCC kids are even finding in some backwaters today), the condition of the Negro had become worse by 1900, in some ways, than it was in 1860.

For a society to condone what is evil is inconceivable: it must be disguised and perhaps portrayed as a positive good. To induce a nation to accept the non-enforcement of the Fifteenth Amendment, its people had to be led to believe that enfranchisement had been unfortunate, even vicious. When inequality was being institutionalized, in violation of the Fourteenth Amendment's assurances of equality, the architects of the Fourteenth Amendment had to be denigrated. This was effectively done by white historians from Rhodes to Bowers (and even later) who depicted the Republican radicals in the language of their foes of the sixties: vindictive, self-seeking, and unscrupulous, or vain theorists who were windbags to boot. They compounded their offense by making Orwellian unpersons of Frederick Douglass and the Southern Negro statesmen who emerged after the Civil War, and the black regiments that helped win the war amendments.

Never had such twin images of evil as the abolitionist and the carpet-bagger been created by historians. This was an essential part of establishing that the Negro was unfit to be a participant in a democracy and of perpetuating that exclusion. Even the bright, young and somewhat "radical" historians who are now helping to demolish the myths about the history of our race relations cannot quite bring themselves to admit that their predecessors were bigots. They indulge in a variety of ingenious speculation and psychologizing in attempted explanation of the injustices that are being eroded by current revisionism.

Justice not only to the Negro but to the white man of integrity and conscience has been the object of the research and agitation of the Negro History Movement. The battle against anti-Negro history turned the corner with the publication in 1935 of W. E. B. DuBois' *Black Reconstruction*, a book that had a shattering impact in its day, and that still has a passionate freshness and vitality that make the current neo-revisionists look pallid. One wonders whether it was a McCarthyite hangover that prevented the reviewers of a most notable recent work from mentioning DuBois (the old man joined the Communist Party at 93 after a flirtation of some years). Furthermore, it was unjust of Stampp, the author of that work, to dismiss *Black Reconstruction* as "naive" and "disappointing." [1]

The Rosenwald Fund aided DuBois' work in the thirties. For the most part, however, even now when everybody wants to be seen in the act, the wealthy foundations that like to be thought of as the "angels" of the Movement and that have been prodigal in grants to way-out poets and the like have not supported the efforts of the A.S.N.L.H. One is prompted to suggest that the reason for the abstention is the truly radical character of the search for the truth in race relations history. The men who control the coffers are likely to conclude that their institutions are not threatened as much by direct action street demonstrations as they would be by a widespread revelation that as a nation we have been living on lies; that what has until now been accepted as the American heritage is permeated with falsehood and mendacity.

In the recent decades of the developing Civil Rights Revolution, the National Association for the Advancement of Colored People, the American Council on Education, the Anti-Defamation League, and others joined the fight that had at the beginning been waged virtually alone by the A.S.N.L.H. (One should say that the street demonstrations and other protests launched by NAACP against the original distribution of *The Birth of a Nation* were a phase of the "Negro History" fight.) The academic community did not respond very promptly, nor did the school administrators whose faults were the most grievous, and whose twin problems—revising curricula and retraining teachers—were almost insuperable. The resistance to change could not last indefinitely in the face of the pressures of national self-criticism.

The pitch of protest from local and state organizations began to break into the white press in the 1960's. In Chicago, in August 1963,

---

[1] One of the most satisfactory evaluations is that of John Hope Franklin in an address, as yet unpublished, delivered at a February 1964 memorial meeting to DuBois that was held at Carnegie Hall:

> Since the publication of *Black Reconstruction* American historiography has not been the same and the study of reconstruction can never be the same again. The mark he left is indeed indelible. One sees in it the beginning of the estrangement that was to become complete before his death. One suspects that the review of this period of the nation's history revealed to him a depth of human perfidy here that left him with a sense of helplessness and hopelessness.

Black Reconstruction was added to the "model" White House library at the suggestion of this writer and has been re-issued in paperback by Meridian Books.

a new note in street demonstrations was struck as the Amistad Society sponsored the picketing of the Chicago Board of Education by 100 students and teachers. Their slogans: "Include the Negro in History," "Is History White?" "We've all been brainwashed." Said one demonstrator: "We want Negro history as part of American history, not as a separate unit." The Berkeley chapter of CORE sponsored a study by six University of California historians whose findings were that the school textbooks most widely used in California contained distortions of history that "help perpetuate and intensify the pattern of racial discrimination." The result, they declared, is to "reinforce notions among whites of their superiority." Carter G. Woodson was about to become a man who overcame, fifteen years after his death.

Recognition of the evils has been followed, ever so slowly, by grudging concessions to some of the demands of the protesters. One notable initial breakthrough was the publication, in response to the protests of the Detroit NAACP chapter, of a seventh-grade pamphlet supplement, "The Struggle for Freedom and Rights: Basic Facts About the Negro in American History." This was followed by the appearance during 1964 of identically titled, lengthy booklets *for teachers* in New York City and the District of Columbia: "The Negro in American History." Patchwork changes have been noted in the new editions of the thick, expensive hardbound publications that provide the profit that explains Wall Street's interest in the textbook industry. (One editor in a top company told me, "We don't call them books; we call them products.")

I have published elsewhere a more detailed critique of the initial three pamphlet supplements, particularly the New York School Board's effort, which questions why and by whom a sentence was inserted praising existing texts, and of the separate and not very equal quality of the effort to date.[2] The principal deficiency of the response until now is the failure to face up to the necessary restructuring (not merely reconstruction) of basic thinking on the subject of what our history is about: a sample of what I mean is that we must look upon Charles Sumner, not Webster/Clay/Calhoun, as the focus of attention for the middle of the nineteenth century.

In the Introduction to his recent *The Anti-Slavery Vanguard*, Martin Duberman found it "depressing" to note that the contemporary

---

[2] See "Tokens of Truth," *Integrated Education*, #13 (February/March 1965), Integrated Education Associates, Chicago, Ill., 60604. The same journal carried the six-Professor Berkeley CORE report, #11, October/November 1964.

writers he presents have often quoted "from past writings and speeches which repeat almost word for word arguments and attitudes still current today." I do not think he would have found it depressing so much as instructive if he had a full sense of the scope and the potential of the "Negro History" idea as an instrument of liberation from the fetters of prejudice produced by past scholarly malpractice. Similarly, I do not find it "depressing" that Charles Edward Russell emphasized, writing in 1910, that poverty was difficult to arouse people about because of its invisibility: "Year in and year out, unless I go to seek them," wrote Russell, "I shall see practically no persons that do not have enough to eat, enough to wear, and are not comfortably housed; for so is the world arranged." His book was entitled *Why I Am a Socialist.* There are significant conclusions to be drawn from the fact that so few liberals or radicals are aware that the concept of the invisibility of poverty is not a recent, sensational discovery.

The thoroughgoing re-excavation of our past that the Negro History lesson should inspire can extend, too, to the virtually unanimous agreement of all the good writers of the country, who united a decade before Russell's book was published, as Van Wyck Brooks has told us, to argue "that America had no right to hold subject states, or to crush a republic—or to take over the title of a dispossessed tyrant." Those who question the involvement of civil rights leaders in the effort to turn toward peace need to be reminded of the militant response of the surviving abolitionists at the turn of the century, in joining the 100% American "Anti-Imperialist League" that came into being to fight the suppression of the Philippine Insurrection.[3]

[3] As instructive as their protest was the response of a Massachusetts pro-Imperialist of 1900 who defended the slaughter of the natives because of the strategic importance of control of the Southeast Asian region in relation to "the richest prize . . . the vast markets of China." His name was Henry Cabot Lodge.

One of the finest personal portraits in the *New York Times* "Man in the News" series was published on March 26, 1965 during the March from Selma to Montgomery. Selected to symbolize the marchers and the Alabama Freedom Fighters who may have begun the ending of the nullification of the Fifteenth Amendment was a Negro named Albert Turner, who had given up a fairly prosperous situation as a bricklayer to go into voter registration work. Interviewed by the *Times,* Mr. Turner was more relevant than I could be in summarizing the need for the truthful integration of America's heritage.

"In school I learned the whiteman's history," Mr. Turner says.

Reconstruction was presented as a bad thing and the fact that there were Negro voters and Negro officials in the Alabama of the eighteen seventies was not mentioned. The youth learned that by outside reading, although he "sort of knew it was true all the time."

"You can learn a lot from history," Mr. Turner says. "We know now that you can't change the political system from above, because it produces leaders that are always trying to sell you wooden nickels. The movement has got to be rooted in the people."

[From Negro Digest, June 1964]

ENRICHED HISTORY FOR THE WHITE MAN

By Howard N. Meyer[1]

"The battle for justice to the Negro in our history is but a part of the battle for justice to the whole truth in our history."

The milling process destroys the vitamins and sucks the minerals out of our flour. For years this resulted in malnutrition in families whose diet centered on bread. Rickety, spavined, pimply or otherwise defective bodies were the consequence. Only when the millers accepted the simple suggestion of some genius that they put back what they'd been taking out was this source of social evil stopped. The restored product was called "enriched" flour.

Honest white scholars have, most of them, come to agree with what Negro scholars have long known. For many decades, reaching back prior to the turn of the century, the school subject that was taught as "American History" wasn't that at all. The vitamins of the contribution of the Negro to our Nation and its heritage and the minerals of the truth about race relations were carefully removed. The effect of the resulting mental malnutrition has been devastating. To the Negro it was destructive of his sense of personal worth, of self-respect, of identity—except when, through family traditions, or by benefiting from the single virtue of a segregated college, he learned some of the truth. To the white it was a calamity: it contributed largely to a corruption of the spirit; rickety and pimply mental and spiritual attitudes were the effect of the bleached history product.

Through the years, an awakening and fighting talented tenth has promoted a subject which, for lack of better name, has been called "Negro History." W.E. B. Du Bois and Carter G. Woodson were the founding fathers of the fight. Until very recently, the work of exploiting their breakthroughs was confined within racial channels. It was almost exclusively the Negro writer, editor, reader, and student who obtained the benefit. The result was separate, and not very equal. It was not the true American heritage; the isolated presentation of the story of the Negro in America was as incomplete in its own way as the story of America without the Negro. Short of the day when the integrated story would be told, two incomplete tales were better than one.

The average American public school has continued to teach the standard bleached product, devitalized, at best in its absence of reference to Negro achievement and participation in American life; poisoned, at worst, in its falsehoods and distortions concerning the role of the Negro in such epochal periods as the abolitionist and the Reconstruction eras.

This is a problem and an evil that has not been sectional. Moreover, during a period when, under the pressure of the Negro revolution, the moral climate has improved somewhat, there has been little mitigation of the faults of the past. In 1934, Professor Lawrence D. Reddick wrote for the Journal of Negro History a study of Southern U.S. history texts. Among his findings: "The place and development of the Negro in the national life since the granting of freedom and citizenship are ignored almost completely. . . . These authors usually depict the Negroes as pawns, passive instruments in the hands of others (during Reconstruction)." In 1961, Dr. Lloyd Marcus compiled for the Anti-Defamation League a study of the treatment of minorities in texts: "The achievements of living Negro Americans are mentioned in very few books. . . . American Negroes are portrayed, for the most part, in the eras of slavery and Reconstruction. What comes through in most books is a stereotype of a simple, childlike, superstitious people. . . ." Thus, what Professor Reddick saw in the Southern school textbooks of the 1930's was found by the B'nai B'rith's researchers to be true on a national scale in 1961.

Lacking in the A.D.L. evaluation is one critical fact: that the Reconstruction Sambo stereotype is the product of gross falsehood, the cumulative result of a libel on a whole people. "Gross falsehood" is a strong phrase, not lightly used by one trained as an attorney to be careful in the choice of words—but it is not my own. It is the phrase of Professor Arnold Rose, co-author with Gunnar Myrdal of "An American Dilemma". As a sociologist whose principal concern has been with "the problem," he has studied and evaluated most U.S. history writings in an effort to get at the roots of bigotry and prejudice in our land. He focuses his attention on this issue in his essay in the new book that he edited, "Assuring Freedom to the Free".

[1] Howard N. Meyer, a New York lawyer, is author of the books "Let Us Have Peace", "Colonel of the Black Regiment" and other essays on human rights.

"And how does it happen," asks Professor Rose, "that most white Americans believe this gross falsehood? It happens because their teachers teach it in the public schools, and the teachers learned it at the teachers' colleges, and the teachers' colleges got it from the professors at the great universities. The professors got it, not out of scholarly researches, but out of the post-Reconstruction apologies for the South written by Negro-haters."

Now a "gross falsehood" is just another way of saying "big lie," and those of us who are old enough to remember Joseph Goebbels know that Hitler's master-propagandist preached and practised the doctrine that a falsehood, repeated often enough, can enslave the minds of men. Those whites whose image of the Negro is derived solely, or primarily, from what they have learned in school histories, are vexed and perplexed today. Taught all their lives to believe in the stereotypes that were created to justify separation and inequality, they find themselves suddenly preached at and told they have been "wrong."

"You've got to be taught to hate and fear," ran the song in Rodgers' and Hammerstein's interracial hit, "South Pacific". "You've got to be carefully taught." Should it surprise us to find that some white resent moving over and making room for—or even extending a friendly hand to—those they were taught to hate? When an individual is libeled—the victim of a malicious falsehood—the law requires retraction or compensation, or both. What is the remedy for decades of libel against a whole people?

"Belatedly, educators are coming to see," said Time magazine, commenting on the District of Columbia's new separate supplemental pamphlet for school history classes, "The Negro in American History," "that it is high time to de-segregate the teaching of U.S. history." Not only is it high time—it is too little and too late. French statesman Georges Clemenceau is supposed to have said that War is much too important to leave to the generals. The need for remedying the misteaching of American History is too vital to leave it to the schools and the teachers. The "educators" have failed us; they have bequeathed to us three generations of white Americans whose many variants of the question, "Why are they pushing so fast?", betrays their ignorance of their own heritage as much as it does their utter lack of moral sense.

There are various schools of psychiatry today, differing theories as to how mental illness should be treated. Most agree that the important objective is to cause the patient to develop insight into his character structure, something most effectively accomplished by re-examination of one's early life so that one can get at the root of false beliefs about himself. The psychiatrist strives to demonstrate the contradiction between the way a situation actually was, and the way the patient thought it was, between the way the patient was behaving and the way he thought he was behaving. The irrational rejection of human beings because of the shade of skin—colorphobia—in the United States, is the greatest case of mass mental illness in the world's history. It cannot be cured by laws alone, nor by simply saying that what was right yesterday is wrong today.

Who is there to do this job that the "educators" have made necessary? This is the hardest part of the fight. As the Negro revolution moved into its decisive phase, Loren Miller correctly pointed out that "Freedom Now-Today" is a slogan that "implies rejection of the dogma that racial reforms must await a change in the hearts and minds of men." What the militants have missed, however, is that those hard hearts must be moved and those warped minds cured. There is nothing sensational, glamorous, or exciting about "history;" the ambitious or publicity-hungry leader sees no percentage in it. They debate in their press releases about the resistance, the white backlash, the need for new tools—and give little attention to the importance of the Freedom Writer to consolidate the gains that the Freedom Rider has achieved.

What is needed, as a weapon to win the Negro revolution *is an adult education program of unimaginably vast proportions.* Its content should neither be called "Negro History" nor constitute merely that. There is a hidden American heritage to be unearthed that can enrich us all. Few white Americans know the magnificent life story of Frederick Douglass; one can return again and again to his writings and find a lesson for today. But the culturally deprived American has not been told of Wendell Phillips either, or been given his magnificent insights into the nature of the relationship between capital and labor.

One perceptive theologian, Professor A. J. Heschel, has likened the 1963 phase of the Negro Revolution to the crossing of the Red Sea by the Israelites. There still remained ahead of them the hardships of the wilderness. The Israelites murmured against Moses in the desert and said, "What shall we drink?" for there was no water. In the same fashion, the Negro will justly cry out after a Civil Rights Bill is passed. "What shall we eat? We want adequate education, decent housing, proper employment.

There are lessons as to how these problems can be solved in the enriched history that we must all learn. The vitamins and minerals that have been removed include not merely the contribution of the Negro to our heritage: Few know the lives and teachings of such great and near-forgotten Americans as Theodore Parker, the Brook Farmers, and the other radical reformers of the abolitionist era, or John Boyle O'Reilly, John Peter Altgeld, and the populists (not all of whom became racists) of the later nineteenth century. The great lesson to be learned is that a "war on poverty" cannot be waged from the top: the poor and the men and women of conscience of the middle class must unite in political action, if the causes of poverty are to be removed.

"Understanding the past," said Arthur Schlesinger Jr. "can be the key to the future." "The past is never dead," says one of William Faulkner's characters. "It is not even past." The present condition of the human race is solely a product of its history; if that condition is to be changed for the better, it can be effectively done only by beginning with a re-examination of that history. We must find out what really happened, as the psychiatrist says, to cure ourselves from the sickness that comes from what we have been deluded into thinking was our past.

When Dr. W. E. B. Du Bois wrote the Declaration of Independence of the Third American Revolution, the Resolutions of the Niagara movement of 1905–6, he said, "The battle we wage is not for ourselves alone, but for all true Americans." Some of the white trash of the North, who have been revealed in the last few months, will never understand this. "There is some folks," said Louis Armstrong once, "that if they don't know, you can't tell 'em." But most Americans can and will come to learn that the Negro Revolution is their own cause. After they have re-learned their history and cast aside the myths and stereotypes they learned in school will they understand they are not merely "doing something for the Negro" when they ally themselves with him.

The battle for justice to the Negro in our history is but a part of the battle for justice to the whole truth in our history. When that is gained, "Ye shall know the truth, and the truth shall make ye free."

[The Wall Street Journal, Friday, February 23, 1968]

W. E. B. DuBois and "The Problem of the Color Line"

By Howard N. Meyer [1]

William Edward Burghardt DuBois was born in Massachusetts a century ago today, shortly before the ratification of the Fourteenth Amendment. He died in Africa at the age of 95, on the eve of the civil rights march on Washington of August 1963, when a quarter million Americans assembled to protest the denial of the Amendment's promises of equality and justice. When asking a moment of silent prayer for the old man, Roy Wilkins told the gathering, "For 60 years his has been the voice that was calling you here today."

Descended from a slave who won freedom as a soldier in the American Revolution, DuBois became the first of his race to win a doctorate at Harvard. He displayed in his earliest publications scholarship in both history and sociology that would surely, had he been white, have led to a long and notable academic career. Repelled by the prospect of indefinite segregation in a Negro college, appalled by the state of race relations at the turn of the century, he could not help but become an activist. Though always an individualist, not having a capacity to mix easily or possessing the common touch, he became a leader by the sheer force of his intellect in the rebirth of militant protest against racism.

While Booker T. Washington still held a one-man monopoly of "black power," after successfully advocating a policy of accommodation, Dr. DuBois called together a small group of Negro intellectuals and businessmen to lead his people along a different path. They started the "Niagara movement," so-called because they met first at Niagara Falls, symbolically to recall the Underground Railroad

[1] The author, a New York attorney, was a special assistant to the U.S. Attorney General under Presidents Roosevelt and Truman. He recently wrote "Colonel of the Black Regiment," a biography of Thomas Wentwork Higginson.

(but on the Canadian side because no hotel on the U.S. side would accept Negro guests in 1905).

This group, which was to help found and to merge itself into the National Association for the Advancement of Colored People, met again in 1906 at Harpers Ferry—another invocation of history—and issued a manifesto. That document, drafted by DuBois, "kindled a flame that, much later, would finally awaken the nation," as Thurgood Marshall, now a Supreme Court Justice, told the 1966 White House Conference on civil rights.

NIAGARA RESOLUTIONS

Those concerned to know "what the Negro wants" have only to turn to the original Niagara resolutions of 1906. "Freedom, manhood, . . . the right to work and the chance to rise" were the themes. They called for full and equal suffrage and the end of segregation. As proof of the introductory passage, "The battle we wage is not for ourselves alone, but for all true Americans," they called for an administration of justice that would be not only color-blind but classless. Decrying the inadequacy of educational opportunity that afflicted poor white as well as poor black they warned: "Either the United States will destroy ignorance or ignorance will destroy the United States."

Present day intellectuals are concerned with a deficiency in public education that lends ominous plausibility to the forecast. Ignorance of the root causes of discontent, past and present, lack of knowledge as to the quality and quantity of Negro contributions to the American culture, society and economy are factors in the apathy that seems once more to be closing in.

A case in point is the ignorance of most Americans concerning the genius, the gifts, the very identity of DuBois. It is to the discredit of the rest of us that only a miniature leftist youth group bears his name.

Although DuBois was a leader, a scholar and a writer, he should above all be remembered as a prophet. By now his most widely quoted forecast, written while McKinley was President and Victoria reigned, has been proved: "The problem of the 20th century is the problem of the color-line—the relation of the darker to the lighter races of men in Asia and Africa, in America and the islands of the sea."

His prophecies that were warnings as well have been insufficiently heeded. In 1903, in a rare confrontation-in-print with Booker T. Washington, he argued the case for higher education for the "talented tenth," but concluded with words still timely: "Men of America, the problem is plain before you. Here is a race transplanted through the criminal foolishness of your fathers. Whether you like it or not the millions are here, and here they will remain. If you do not lift them up, they will pull you down."

"LITTLE TO LOSE"

The Presidential Commission that is attempting to answer the question, "Where did we go wrong?" might study the context of the prophecy that concluded DuBois' masterwork, "Black Reconstruction." He wrote in 1935 that the Negro's "frustration cannot indefinitely continue. Some day it may burst in fire and flood. Who will be to blame? And where the greater cost? Black folk, after all, have little to lose, but civilization has all."

Until the publication of DuBois' massive re-examination of the Reconstruction era the almost unanimously accepted version of the history of the period deprecated the architects of the Civil Rights Amendments to the Constitution and their beneficiaries. The conscious or unconscious purpose and clear effect of that tradition was, as Arnold Rose, co-author of "An American Dilemma," was the first to point out, precisely like the technique of the dictator depicted in Orwell's "Nineteen Eighty Four," who controlled the motivations of human beings by manipulating their beliefs about their past. Gradually, since the publication of "Black Reconstruction," the substance of its author's critique of the previously dominant academic view has won wide acceptance.

The continent where he died has been more generous to the memory of DuBois than his native land. A confidential State Department survey showed him to be, shortly before his death, the American best known and most popular among African intellectuals. This was not primarily due to his eminence among American Negroes. When Africa was still under colonial rule, it was DuBois who founded the first Pan African Congress in Paris in 1919. Through this group he furnished inspiration for the efforts of African nationalists that came to fruition during the last decade.

In 1945 DuBois was named by President Truman to be one of the group that attended with Ralph Bunche at the San Francisco founding of the United Nations. Had he died shortly afterward he might be honored today with the standard array of centennial tributes. For example, commemorative postage stamps have thrice been granted Booker T. Washington but denied DuBois (yet not withheld from Robert E. Lee or Stonewall Jackson).

The services rendered his country by DuBois are now ignored, as if in punitive retribution for the political deviations of his last 15 years. In some cases, erased: In the 1947 edition of "Inside U.S.A." John Gunther found DuBois to be a 20th century figure to be compared only to Shaw and Einstein; in the enlarged 1951 edition of the same work that reference was omitted.

The old man's principal offense was to align himself with the advocates of abolition of atomic war, perhaps not unwisely, but too soon, like the premature antifascists of a decade earlier. Coupled with this was his expression of opposition to our stance in the cold war, another era whose history is even now being re-examined and rewritten. At the age of 83 he was arrested and indicted as an alleged unregistered agent of a foreign principal; the prosecution collapsed when a Federal judge found the case too flimsy to submit to a jury. Embittered and further alienated, he surprised few when he joined the Communist Party at the age of 93. Since the announcement was made at the time the penalties of the McCarran Act were being invoked, his action may have been more a gesture of defiance of a ruling that was later to be held to be unconstitutional.

The last of the prophecies that we seem fated to ignore was contained in his account of the events that led to his arrest, prosecution and acquittal. "The moral basis of military training and its ethical standards must revolve about murder and destruction and can never normally grasp social uplift and human progress. For this reason all civilizations of the past have sedulously avoided the rule of soldiers save as a fatal last resort."

TIMELY APPRAISAL

NEW YORK.

EDITOR, THE WALL STREET JOURNAL.

Howard N. Meyer's article "W.E.B. Du Bois and 'The Problem of the Color Line'" (Feb. 23) is a perceptive and timely appraisal of the man who, more than any other single individual, shaped the modern Negro protest movement. Essentially an intellectual he was also an activist leader.

It is ironic and highly significant that of the major New York newspapers only The Wall Street Journal saw fit to notice Dr. Du Bois' centennial. It was not that the other newspapers were uninformed about the observance; it was that they chose to ignore it. But despite the snub, Dr. Du Bois' historic contributions to the struggle for human freedom will long be cherished not only by people of African descent everywhere, but also by knowledgeable non-Negroes who believe in equality, justice and freedom for all.

HENRY LEE MOON,
Editor, The Crisis.

NATIONAL CATHOLIC CONFERENCE FOR INTERRACIAL JUSTICE,
Chicago, Ill., March 13, 1968.

Hon. JAMES H. SCHEUER,
House of Representatives,
Washington, D.C.

DEAR CONGRESSMAN SCHEUER: The National Catholic Conference for Interracial Justice heartily endorses your proposed Commission on Negro History and Culture as outlined in H.R. 12962. It would serve as a catalyst for development of creative uses of already existing documents, books, and artifacts of Negro culture as well as a national library and archival center for Negro history. Precious historical materials are being lost due to lack of coordination in assembling, curating, codifying, and discovering Negro cultural documentary material. We also urge you to include aspects of African art and Negro-American art as part of your efforts because the art of man reflects man himself and contributes to his search for self-image.

While it is true that some significant progress is apparent in the integration of school teaching tools, principally textbooks, only a beginning has been made. Your proposed H.R. 12962 Bill providing for this Commission on Negro History and Culture would provide national leadership for overcoming a grievous omission in the full and complete heritage of both white and black Americans.

Sincerely yours,

MATHEW AHMANN, *Executive Director.*

○